Ben Waddington

CW00553436

111 Pla
in Birming ....
That You
Shouldn't Miss

Photographs by Janet Hart

emons:

For Roxie

MIX
Paper from
responsible sources
FSC® C043106

© Emons Verlag GmbH
All rights reserved
© Photographs by Janet Hart, except see p. 238
© Cover Icon: shutterstock.com/Leka Leck
Layout: Eva Kraskes, based on a design
by Lübbeke | Naumann | Thoben
Maps: velovia, www.velovia.bike,
Frank Ullrich & Kristof Halasz
© OpenStreetMap contributors
Editing: Martin Sketchley
Printing and binding: Grafisches Centrum Cuno, Calbe
Printed in Germany 2023
ISBN 978-3-7408-1350-5
First edition

Guidebooks for Locals & Experienced Travellers
Join us in uncovering new places around the world at
www.111places.com

Foreword

Welcome to Birmingham, city of industry, creativity and ingenuity, of super-diverse culture, piquant tastes, hard work and vigour, canals and cars, heavy metal, and of blushing self-effacement. This is a city having many identities down the centuries, beginning as a humble market town before rising as an international hub of science and industry, and a destination of full employment for people of many cultures. Post-war Birmingham revealed a bold but shell-shocked city with a vision to rebuild as a car utopia. In more recent years, seemingly embarrassed by its industrial, power-hungry past, and in bull-headed pursuit of second city status, it has variously presented itself as a hub of shopping, conferences, regeneration and cuisine.

Yet there are still undercurrents that recognise and assert the value of Birmingham's bold, creative spirit. This restless character, the serial rebranding and ceaseless rebuilding can make Birmingham a challenge to pin down. The chapters that follow have been chosen to reveal the city's curious character, the Birmingham that reaches beyond the utilitarian, the humble and the brusque. Here are the subtle clues to the city's productive past and vibrant present, and which look towards a more sustainable future. Expect inconspicuous museums, cryptic details, sacred sites, public art, industrial remnants, myths, cool bars, spirits, demons and imposing landscapes.

This book defiantly exceeds Birmingham's city limits, making regular forays into the neighbouring boroughs and regions of Solihull, Sutton Coldfield and the Black Country to tell that wider story. Please note too that several places listed here open infrequently and require your most determined scheduling. Researching and writing this book highlighted not only just how unexplored Birmingham is, but also how enjoyable, inspiring, jarring and unique. Now, go and discover!

111 Places

1 Anchor Exchange
Cold War era tunnel system

Looming over the back lots and car parks just outside the Inner Ring Road is a tall brick structure topped with slotted vents. This is Anchor Exchange Shaft 2, and the service lift into a secret network of tunnels running beneath the city.

The system is less of a state secret now than when it was excavated in 1957, intended then as an underground telephone exchange that could maintain communications in Birmingham even after a nuclear attack. These days, it is still an exchange of sorts, as this is where BT runs the telecommunication cables that power the city's internet connection. For security reasons, this is still pretty hush-hush, but there is plenty of overground evidence of the tunnels to keep surface-dwellers intrigued. The now-dormant BT Tower on Lionel Street is the most prominent of these clues. Graffiti in the car park gives fellow urban explorers a heads up: 'Tunnels close by – Anchor Exchange'. The name Anchor Exchange is derived from the jewellery hallmarking symbol for Birmingham.

A similar shaft in the same pink brick can be glimpsed from the back of Thorpe Street car park, formerly the drill hall of Warwickshire Rifle Volunteers. This shaft is shallower, as the tunnels are now much closer to the surface. At the height of the Cold War, the tunnels were fully equipped for subterranean life, including a canteen and pool tables to keep a skeleton staff fed and occupied. The tunnels were put on amber alert during the Cuban Missile Crisis of 1962, but by that point advances in nuclear bomb technology meant the tunnels were unlikely to survive a direct attack.

The shaft serves as a lasting reminder of international political tensions and what can happen when we stop communicating. Unfortunately, the only way to see any of this is to train as a BT engineer specialising in broadband fibre optics and to apply for a transfer to Birmingham.

Address Visible from Lionel Street Car Park, 21 Lionel Street, Birmingham B3 1AT |
Getting there Five-minute walk from the city centre | Tip The former Assay Office is a
splendid Victorian Italianate building at 143 Newhall Street.

2   The Angry Wall

A towering wall of mysterious cylinders

Highbury Park's more usual entrances are at Alcester Street and Shutlock Lane. Entering from Yew Tree Road will bring you to the lesser-known pinetum and Italian Garden. But enter the park via a leafy alley off Queensbridge Road, next to the Uffculme estate's lodge house, and you'll discover the curious Angry Wall. You won't miss it: the wall is 20 feet high, and comprises around 2,000 stacked cylinders, four feet long and made from a rough ceramic.

For much of its life, however, the wall was lost, becoming overgrown with ivy until the foliage was trimmed back in 2007. Over the course of the intervening decades, the original purpose of the wall was forgotten, and its discovery prompted the emergence of folkloric interpretations. What is clear is that the wall is a densely wooded boundary between two large estates: Uffculme, being the 1890 home of the chocolatier Richard Cadbury, and Highbury, being the residence of the local statesman Joseph Chamberlain. The popular story was that the fired clay cylinders represented canon shells, stacked and ready for use in the Boer Wars, and an endorsement by Chamberlain of those conflicts. Knowingly, this was to insult the peace-loving sensibilities of the Quaker Cadbury family. Others have suggested that these are the actual shell casings, returned from battle. However, no feud was known to exist between the two families, and such a spiteful gesture would have come at enormous expense.

The true story here is probably one of early industrial recycling. Research by Jim Andrew for The Chamberlain Highbury Trust identifies the cylinders as a type of crucible for heat treatment in metal manufacture, a strong, solid form that can be reused in landscaping projects. Other examples of this recycling can be spotted around the city. The Angry Wall, now referred to as the Crucible Wall, was likely a soundproofing measure against the Cadbury's outdoor social gatherings by the peace-loving Chamberlains.

Address Entrance off Queensbridge Road, Moseley, Birmingham B13 8QY | Getting there Bus 35 or 50 to Kings Heath | Tip Cross over Alcester Road and turn left towards Ambler Brothers Funeral Services to find an old retaining wall made entirely of repurposed blast furnace slag.

3___Apple Tree

How do you like them apples?

How many varieties of English apple can you name? You'll know a few found in supermarkets: Bramley, Cox, Spartan… In fact over 2,000 varieties exist, although most remain untasted and unknown outside specialist orchards or farmers' markets. The Romans first brought apples to England, and through the Georgian and Victorian eras, many new varieties were cultivated. Fruit trees appeared as standard in the gardens of domestic properties. Perhaps the assumption is that wild apples are either hard, sour and only suitable for cooking, or soft but inedibly docile.

However, the finicky supermarket selector has given a false impression of the many edible varieties available, and perhaps because apple trees look rather gnarly they are uncommonly selected when populating the green civic spaces of the city. A row of trees on Selly Avenue running alongside the park provides a rare option to tempt more adventurous fruit pickers.

Laced with lichens, these weathered specimens produce a small but delicious apple from September, and remind us of a period when the city's civic tree wardens more actively endorsed sustainability. The trees are also a reminder that we should occasionally explore the edible properties of our everyday environment. If the apples display obvious asymmetry, it underlines the wasteful fussiness of the corporate fruiterer, and the enticing russet shade may have a rougher texture than is preferred by daintier tongues.

However, this apple is all about its flesh, which is crisp, cool, bittersweet, and a surprising shade of pink that seems to have come from a fairy tale. How best to access this fruit, if you arrive in season? If lucky, simply pick low-hanging fruit, or gently tug at a sprig to dislodge higher samples. Bring a dexterous friend who can catch and share the fruits of your labours. Don't eat the windfall apples!

Address Selly Avenue, Selly Park, Birmingham B29 7PE | Getting there Bus 45 or 47 to Kensington Road, then a nine-minute walk | Tip The park and surrounding streets were once the haunt of the poet W H Auden, who lived at 59 Selly Wick Road.

4 The Archery

World's oldest lawn tennis club

As early as 1859, Harry Gem and his friend Augurio Perera created a forerunner of lawn tennis in the garden of the latter's home in nearby Ampton Road, Edgbaston. They knew it first as Pelota (Spanish for 'ball') then later 'lawn rackets' before settling on 'lawn tennis'. The game had even earlier forerunners away from the grass, and Henry VIII was active in the sport that became retrospectively known as 'real tennis'.

In the early 1870s, the game was embraced by Edgbaston Archery Society, where Gem was a member, and who incorporated Lawn Tennis into their title as the popularity of the sport grew. Archery was quietly dropped, although the club was still referred to as The Archery and the sport still appears in the club's full title today: Edgbaston Archery and Lawn Tennis Society. The six lawn courts still occupy their original space, making it the world's oldest continuously open tennis club; a blue plaque records the triumph. Over the years, lawn tennis ever increased in popularity, at least partially because it was a great way to actively meet the opposite sex. Tennis whites emerged as an aesthetic solution to hiding the inevitable sweat.

Today, EALTS remains a popular club in a beautiful setting, benefitting from its verdant neighbour, the Botanical Gardens. The six grass courts are still intact and are now matched by six clay, shale and AstroTurf courts to suit your playing preference. The club is a popular choice with students at the nearby University, and the club offers coaching for players at all skill levels. Most players here have annual memberships, but a deal may be brokered for those staying in Birmingham for a shorter time. While there is no spectator space for non-members, an unofficial view of the courts can be achieved from a suitable bench in the Botanical Gardens immediately next door, and discreetly enjoying the action.

Address 14a Westbourne Road, Edgbaston, Birmingham B15 3TR, www.clubspark.lta.org.uk | Getting there Bus 23 to Harborne Road | Hours Courts may be booked during daylight hours | Tip Dedicated tennis fans should make the journey to Warstone Lane Cemetery in the Jewellery Quarter, where the grave of Harry Gem was recently rediscovered and restored in the cemetery's western end.

5 Argent Centre
Multi-coloured Romanesque

It never seems to appear on calendars, postcards, fridge magnets or montages of iconic Birmingham buildings, but the Argent Centre (originally the Albert Works) is surely one of Birmingham's most striking buildings. Perhaps trying to shake the associations of his name, J G Bland designed this dazzling stack of workshops for W E Wiley, maker of gold pen nibs for the world's most discerning writers.

Sometime before 1862 Bland had surely visited Florence, which is noted for its buildings featuring multi-coloured brick patterns, and recreated the style for the Jewellery Quarter. Indeed, Italy has consistently been an inspiration for Birmingham architects over the years. The red, white and blue bricks also echo the Union Flag, and may have been an Empirical gesture. For all its playful styling, the form is a huge, no-nonsense block. Entering the courtyard shows that its solidity is something of an illusion, the building revealed to be an L-shape of workshops that admit light from both sides to facilitate careful work. In an inspired gesture of early sustainability, the original works incorporated a Turkish steam bath near the chimney on the north side, which redirected steam from the pen-making machines to mellow out stressed Victorian jewellery workers. Sadly, like the H B Sale building (see ch. 55), the structure gained a featureless extra brick wall on the upper level sometime in the 20th century.

Comparing the Argent Centre and other factories of the Jewellery Quarter to those found in Digbeth, while both are principally metal-working areas, those of the Jewellery Quarter are definitely finer. Here, the impression conveyed to customers regarding the design, finesse and care put into production of jewellery was of high importance, whereas rougher, tougher Digbeth was more about robustness, precision and competitive cost.

Address 60 Frederick Street, Birmingham B1 3HS, +44 (0)121 236 9834,
www.penmuseum.org.uk | Getting there Bus 101 to Frederick Street | Hours Tue–Sat
11am–4pm, Sun 1–4pm | Tip The Pen Museum is incorporated into the Argent Centre,
a compact but important collection of pen nib machines and products from a time when
Birmingham was the nib hub of the world.

6 __ Ashley Building
A Brutalist Tower of Babel

Through the years, the University of Birmingham's architecture has mirrored that of the city centre, with bold red brick Victoriana meeting Brutalist interventions, ring roads and retro-futuristic aerial walkways. The University has been more nurturing of its Modernist creations than can be said of the city centre. One joyful highlight is the Ashley Building, which is a five-storey tower of stacked, projecting window modules, construction of which was completed in 1964.

The Ashley Building came at a time when the rotunda was trending as a contemporary architectural form, and when structural building techniques allowed new design possibilities. A new generation of architects began to play, and some of Birmingham's other round buildings are highlighted in this book. What may look cylindrical as you approach appears to change shape as you walk around it. Seen from above, it resembles a snail shell, or perhaps a giant comma.

The building now contains the offices of the university's languages department, and knowing this may bring to mind the Tower of Babel as depicted by Breugel: the tower celebrating the diversity of languages rather than confusion. Despite concrete's reputation for being a bleak and unforgiving material, the Ashley Building is Brutalist Modernism at its most playful. Its angular window cases are offset by the strange and beautiful curves. A helical staircase in concrete provides the fire escape route, and hints at the snail shell inspiration.

The building is closed to the public, but another spiral staircase climbs the inner circumference wall of the building. The inner structure is expressed by the beam ends that appear like spacer blocks between the floors, designed to direct rainwater away. The Ashley Building responds to the Strathcona building next door, which seems to have uncoiled in a long, graceful curve.

ASHLEY BUILDING

Address Ashley Building, University of Birmingham, Edgbaston, Birmingham B15 2TT |
Getting there Train from New Street to University, then an eight-minute walk | Tip More
1960s Brutalism stands nearby with the University's Muirhead Tower, actually two offset
towers, completed in 1971.

7 Asian Fashion Mile

Bridal boutiques and textile bazaars from the East

Stratford Road in Sparkbrook is better known for being one side of the Balti Triangle, the cluster of curry restaurants offering the best place to find the locally-invented dish. However, for many this is a destination in its own right for an entirely different reason: the UK Asian fashion industry has boomed in recent years and this vibrant economy is apparent to anyone who walks the stretch of Stratford Road between Walford Road and Showell Green Lane.

A wealth of independent shops, boutiques and bazaars located here sell Eastern bridal wear, exquisite fashions and colourful textiles. Customers travel many miles to get the UK's best selection of clothes and fabrics to suit a range of budgets. Over the years, outlets have become increasingly lavish to compete for attention. Visitors to Stratford Road don't need to be in the market for sumptuous wedding or party wear to enjoy the richness of colours, patterns, textures and designs that rival the Balti district for sheer sensory stimulation. Each outlet has its own approach to making the best use of light, space and colour to catch attention. Several shops have a second storey of ornately costumed window mannequins facing the street. It is through the wedding outlets that Stratford Road is at its most dazzling. The groom is often as flamboyantly dressed as the bride, with heavily embellished sherwani (long-sleeved outer coats worn by men in South Asia) and embroidered tuxedos competing with the women's extraordinarily lavish creations.

Many shops have floor-to-ceiling rolls of unstitched silks and patterned fabrics, and most boutiques offer tailoring and alteration services to adapt favourite outfits from previous years. The shops appear along both sides of the main road, totalling around a mile of walking, during which visitors are able to get a clear sense of how traditional designs have been both maintained and updated for the 21st century.

Address Stratford Road, Sparkhill between Walford Road and Showell Green Lane, Birmingham B11 | Getting there Bus 2, 3, 4, 5 or 6 to Stratford Road | Tip On the corner of Stratford Road and Baker Street is The Antelope, a former M&B pub complete with sundial and splendid stone relief carving by William Bloye, illustrating the pub's name.

8   Austin Village
A clue in kit form to a country at war

A sign on The Oak Walk welcomes you to The Austin Village. Appropriately, it reads 'A unique area, please drive carefully' underneath Austin's curious winged wheel logo. Founded by Herbert Austin in 1905, Austin was an enduring car manufacturer based in Longbridge through most of the 20th century. The village itself dates back to 1917, and was a quick solution to accommodating a sudden influx of workers at the plant. Car production was already increasing and attracting workers, but it was the escalation of the First World War that meant extra hired hands were required to make tanks and aircraft.

The village pre-empts the larger scale use of prefabs seen during the Second World War to replace bombed houses, as seen on Wake Green Road (see ch. 89). Austin Village is made up of 250 prefabricated bungalows shipped in from American mail-order home company, Aladdin. The bungalows are made of cedar wood, and indeed many of the street names (Cedar Way, Walnut Way, Elder Close and Maple Way) refer to popular American trees. Even the local pub is called The Woodpecker. The wooden bungalows are interspersed with several brick-built semi-detached houses that act as fire breaks in case of disaster. The village is laid out in a symmetrical pattern that, seen from above, resembles the upright radiator grille of cars from this period.

Over a century later, the bungalows are still standing, much loved by their occupants and forming a close-knit community. What were once identical kit houses have over the years assumed some of the character of their owners, who have lightly modified fences, roofs and gardens. An early adaption was to install a chimney outside the bungalow, and the inevitable creation of driveways for cars. When the village became a conservation area, many of these changes were seen as detrimental to the village's character – a hazard of residing in a living museum.

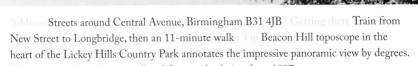

Address Streets around Central Avenue, Birmingham B31 4JB · Getting there Train from New Street to Longbridge, then an 11-minute walk · Tip Beacon Hill toposcope in the heart of the Lickey Hills Country Park annotates the impressive panoramic view by degrees. The toposcope is set in a crenellated faux castle, dating from 1907.

9 Bacchus Bar
Portal to a time-travelling fantasia

Enter the mysterious realm of Bacchus Bar, situated beneath the Burlington Hotel, and prompting imaginative transportations for those locals who have discovered the venue since it first appeared in the 1970s. Landlords Nicholsons have three other traditional pubs in Birmingham that celebrate local history, but the Bacchus Bar goes several steps further, with its themed set pieces, acknowledging the bar's proximity to the former Theatre Royal on New Street (The Shakespeare round the corner does this too).

From Burlington Arcade, there is only the sly presence of a pagan green man by the menu to indicate something is afoot below. A lift or steps take you down to the entrance to the diversely time-zoned bar and restaurant. You will immediately notice sumptuous oil paintings, frescos, antiques, wrought ironwork and tapestries in the flickering lights. As with all theatre, a closer look reveals the artifice of the props. Many cultures, artefacts and eras are referenced in this post-modern potpourri of rooms and spaces, but common to them all is the presence of Bacchus, Roman god of wine and fertility, inducer of drunkenness and religious ecstasy. The hall is dressed in pageantry, and a suit of armour stands guard, referencing New Street's medi-aeval origins.

The vaulted ceiling here is one of the interior's few authentic fea-tures. Turn right, and find yourself in an Egyptian burial chamber, Horus and hieroglyphs moulded in plaster on the walls. Left, and you are in a Victorian library, with moulded ceiling, its walls dense with bound volumes and evoking the study of Sherlock Holmes. The restaurant area beyond returns to classical themes. A modern dropped ceiling breaks away to reveal partially visible ceiling panels and painted frescos. It is possible to find a cosy nook to suit your taste and expectations, the windowless environment helping to maintain your fantasy.

Address Burlington Arcade, New Street, Birmingham B2 4JH, +44 (0)121 632 5445, www.nicholsonspubs.co.uk | Getting there Train to New Street or buses to the city centre | Hours Mon–Fri noon–11pm, Sat 11am–11pm, Sun noon–10pm | Tip Cocktail-mixing neighbour Tonight Josephine occupies the next cellar along on Stephenson Street, celebrating the life of Napoleon's lover and offering a dazzling neon background for you to enjoy your Rum Bongo.

10 Back to Backs Museum
Throw them up, pack them in

Back-to-back houses show the downside of life in a thriving industrial city. How to accommodate the new workers arriving in the 19th century, many of whom were on a low wage? The answer was to speedily erect terraced houses, partitioned down the middle, often arranged around a court. The result was unhygienic, ill-lit and very high-density living. The National Trust's Back to Backs museum on Inge Street illustrates the daily life and work of the families who lived here, in rooms so compact that a visit can only be made by a timed guided tour for a few people at once.

The cluster of buildings began in 1810 with an ordinary house featuring an impressive inglenook fireplace and scullery. In 1821, this was converted into a back-to-back pair, and other such pairs appeared afterwards, forming an L-shape. Those on Hurst Street are perhaps the most compact city living solutions most people will ever see. Several trades operated from the court, and the museum recreates the minuscule workshops of a clock hand cutter and a glass eye maker.

A Public Health Act of 1875 put an end to the building of further back-to-backs, but incredibly the houses here (and across the UK) were still occupied up until the 1960s. In 1966, the BBC screened Ken Loach's *Cathy Come Home*, raising awareness of a problem unknown to many, and bringing about a change in social attitudes to uninhabitable housing and homelessness. The TV play was set in London, but some scenes were filmed in Birmingham as the city offered a level of squalor not seen in London. Coincidentally, the homeless charity Shelter launched a few days later, which led to wide-spread slum clearances.

The museum represents the last surviving back-to-back court in Birmingham. The museum (incorporating – with a spirit of irony – holiday flats) was opened in 2004, and acknowledges the importance and appeal of ordinary people's stories.

Address 55–63 Hurst Street/50–54 Inge Street, Birmingham B5 4TE, +44 (0)121 454 5922, www.nationaltrust.org.uk/birmingham-back-to-backs | **Getting there** Train to New Street, then a five-minute walk; bus 61 or 63 to Smallbrook Queensway | **Hours** Thu–Sun 10am–4pm by pre-booked tour only | **Tip** The dramatic entrance to the car park on Thorpe Street, complete with pastiche crenellations and arrow-slits, was once the doorway to the Warwickshire Rifle Volunteers drill hall.

11 The Bartons Arms

Showboating Minton Hollins opulence

The Bartons Arms looks rather marooned, situated next to the busy A 34 in Newtown, and with not a single Victorian ally anywhere nearby. Its size and the four-faced clock tower suggest aspirations to being a civic building, but its isolation only serves to make it a dignified survivor. Birmingham boasts several flamboyant, red brick boozers styled by the architects James & Lister Lea, but The Bartons Arms' uniqueness is in its interior, designed by the widely-admired Staffordshire tiling company, Minton Hollins. No colour scheme exists as such, but seemingly every single pattern, colour and size of tile in the company's 1901 repertoire is worked into the interior design somewhere, and represents Victorian overbearing opulence at its height. See if you can spot the small tile bearing the Minton Hollins stamp.

This is a particularly well-preserved pub, with original stained glass windows inside and out, elaborately engraved mirrors, and frosted-glass snob screens – a row of rotating windows in the upper part of the bar that meant the publican did not get to look at those he was serving too closely. An extravagant wrought iron staircase invites further exploration of the building, up to what was once the billiard room. The pub's splendour is perhaps explained by the Aston Hippodrome, which once stood next door: The Bartons Arms was originally that theatre and music hall's green room. Singers, dancers and performers visited after – and perhaps before – their shows. Famous customers include Charlie Chaplin, Laurel and Hardy, and once-local regular Ozzy Osbourne.

Today the pub serves a tasteful selection of craft beers and ales, as well as Thai food in the restaurant. The staff host their own guided tour, history talk and dinner combination events, and there are regular performances by live bands in the upstairs section in the evenings.

Address 144 High Street, Aston, Birmingham B6 4UP, +44 (0)121 333 5988, www.thebartonsarms.com | Getting there Bus 7 to Alma Street | Hours Mon–Sat noon–11pm, Sun noon–10pm | Tip Aston Hall, a 20-minute walk away and with an entrance on Upper Thomas Street, is an inspiring Jacobean mansion set in a landscaped garden that surely influenced the designers of The Bartons Arms.

12 Bell Edison Building
Victorian hi-tech communication

You might wonder what this building used to be. It looks important, so you might reach the conclusion that it was a museum, bank, law court, civic building, or perhaps a school. Seeing the name on the brass plaque – 'The Exchange' – you might wonder whether this was a corn exchange, or possibly a stock exchange (Birmingham had both). There is little to indicate that this is a Victorian telephone exchange, built for the National Telephone Company in 1897 for Birmingham's 5,000 subscribers. It's a rich, red fantasia in terracotta, that grows ever more adventurous as the eye moves upwards.

The architects, Martin & Chamberlain, referenced mediaeval and Jacobean styling with Gothic touches: snarling grotesques, louche fish-tailed leopards relaxing on balconies, culminating in pepper-pot turrets at the roofline. The huge foliate roundels in the upper reaches answer those of the nearby School of Art, which was designed by the same architects. Only the Victorian Law Courts surpass this degree of enrichment in Birmingham, which shows the veneration afforded to the new telephone technology. Perhaps because its lower floors are relatively subdued, passers-by tend to miss the extravagant upper details, but this would have been an astounding encounter for any Victorian visitor to the city's business district.

The name of the company appears in tiling in the porch, behind wrought iron gates threaded with poppies. Birmingham was unable to rely on its local stone for its buildings, a pink sandstone that crumbled rather too easily to convey the sense of solidity and permanence architects wanted for their buildings. The prevalent use of red brick and terracotta in this area of the city – sometimes referred to as Birmingham Gothic – is perhaps a proxy for the fragile stone: an industrial solution to a geological problem.

Address The Exchange, 17–19 Newhall Street, Birmingham B3 3PJ | Getting there Train to Snow Hill, then a five-minute walk; bus 22 or 23 | Tip A fine example of Venetian Gothic by J H Chamberlain can be found at Flower and Sons, 132 Edmund Street: sea monsters peer over the cornice, while barley, hops and a cartoon-like flower adorn the porch of the former brewery headquarters.

13 Birmingham Bike Foundry
Recycling since 2010

Over the years, Birmingham has had a wavering relationship with bicycles. For many years bicycles and powered vehicles coexisted happily. Indeed, the manufacture of both accounted for a large proportion of the local economy. In post-war remodelling, however, the city rejected cycling as being outdated and having no place in its future. Yet, after many years of petro-capitalism, the value of cycling is being appreciated once more.

Birmingham Bike Foundry grew from Stirchley's longstanding refurb economy: many citizens head here to repair a failing laptop or broken vacuum cleaner, in a rejection of modern society's throwaway culture. Bike Foundry has an ethos which goes beyond merely selling second-hand cycles, and promotes cycling as a longer-term transport solution rather than a mere leisure activity. When it was set up in 2010, Bike Foundry wanted to remove the barriers to cycling people may have, such as many finding a new bike unaffordable, lacking knowledge of regular maintenance, or not being skilled in making repairs. Unusually for a cycle repair shop, Bike Foundry trains customers to make repairs themselves through initiatives such as Tool Club. Furthermore, its stock comes from refurbishing, tuning up and making roadworthy derelict and abandoned bikes: since opening, it has put 2,000 machines back on the road. Many unusual old bikes turn up as donations after locals clear out their sheds.

Although overshadowed by the car, Birmingham was traditionally a hub for the nation's cycle industry, and Bike Foundry continues this by making bespoke frames to suit customers' individual needs. The policy is currently 'no' to scooters and motorbikes, but the Foundry will soon embrace the rise of the electric bike. The shop also has occasional cycling-themed film screenings in its upstairs space and is active in local community culture.

Address 1539 Pershore Road, Stirchley, Birmingham B30 2JH, www.birminghambikefoundry.org | **Getting there** Bus 45 or 47 to Stirchley; train to Bournville; cycle along National Cycle Route 5 | **Hours** Mon–Fri 10am–6pm, Sat 10am–6pm | **Tip** The Bike Foundry is a workers' co-operative and there are two other shops worth a visit that are also self-managed by their workers: Loaf bakery and cookery school and Artefact café and art gallery, both on Pershore Road.

14 Birmingham Board Schools
Beacons of the future

The board schools of Birmingham are curious architectural interlopers in the city's skylines amongst the spires, turrets, minarets, domes and stupas. In the 1860s, board schools reflected the growing municipal spirit, which also saw the rise of libraries, hospitals, recreation and domestic utilities.

The city sought to improve the environments of its citizens, a movement known in Birmingham as Civic Gospel. Schools were freed from the influence of the religious institutions that many of them resembled, and were free to attend. The schools' distinctive towers were actually ventilation systems, with natural air movement generated by solar power. Most were designed by Martin & Chamberlain, a firm well-versed in giving utilitarian structures an air of reverence. This is Birmingham Gothic: a brash interpretation of Gothic Revival in red brick and terracotta, gleefully unapologetic in its defiance of harmony and constraint.

The schools would have appeared exotic and jarring in the city's prosperous but unexceptional streets. Waverley Road School and Somerville Primary School both have ventilation towers like power stations, brutal and unforgiving in their design, yet with subtle enrichments. Tilton Girls' School has kept its strange octagonal tower despite the spire being lost during the Second World War. Cooksey Road School offers a cartoon-like haunted house of a tower, windowless and foreboding, while the slate cone above Garrison Lane Nursery resembles a witch's hat. Pictured opposite is the sprawling mountain range of Icknield Street School, its three-stage slate peak has created its own language of Gothic.

Sherlock Holmes provides the title 'Beacons of the future' in the story *The Naval Treaty*: 'Light-houses, my boy! Beacons of the future! Capsules with hundreds of bright little seeds in each, out of which will spring the wise, better England of the future'.

Address Icknield Street, Hockley, Birmingham B18 | **Getting there** Bus 16 Platinum or 74 to Hockley Circus | **Tip** The small brick house adjacent to Icknield Street School, now in poor condition, was once the residence of the headmaster.

15 _ Birmingham Opera Company

Nomadic urban explorers

You won't find an opera house in Birmingham, but it does have an opera company. If you can coincide your stay with one of their events, or certainly if you live in the city, you'll experience how Birmingham does culture on its own terms.

Birmingham Opera Company: how opera might look having been banned by a future dystopia, driven underground and played out in derelict sheds on the edge of town by dedicated cultural custodians and an army of volunteers. Since 1987, the company has shown how not being tied to a venue can be a strength, and allow a new art form to emerge. Originally a touring company, they went on to seek such temporary venues as shopping centres, a big-top circus tent, empty industrial spaces, abandoned rock venues and a burnt-out ice rink. They then focussed on opera's drama, atmosphere and heightened emotion, leaving behind the opulent surroundings, expensive seats and champagne bars that may disenfranchise many audiences.

As the company's stages explore the city's urban spaces, so too do audiences, following the action as it moves around. The movement makes the audience a part of the drama: you might find yourself standing next to someone who turns out to be part of the chorus. And you can get closer still, as they recruit hundreds of volunteers to sing and act alongside the professional cast.

The company is behind many innovations in opera and regularly wins major international opera awards. It took until 2009 for the first black tenor to play Othello but it was Birmingham Opera Company that first presented this. Stockhausen's *Mittwoch Aus Licht*, with four helicopters and a camel, was thought to be unstageable, until it was deployed in Digbeth in 2012. Tickets tend to sell out quickly, so make sure you're on the mailing list to experience the next adventure.

Address www.birminghamopera.org.uk | Hours Regular events throughout the year at unexpected locations | Tip Several Birmingham festivals have taken BOC's lead and stage events in adventurous locations, a notable example being the live art and performance festival Fierce, which appears annually (www.wearefierce.org).

16 Bishop Asbury Cottage
The best known Black Country museum in America

Several times a year, American tourists make the long journey to a small cottage in Great Barr to pay homage to a minister who preached in the frontier towns of a newly independent USA. Few people in Birmingham know his name, but in his adoptive homeland Francis Asbury became a bold and influential figure, travelling thousands of miles annually, and becoming one of the first bishops of the popular Methodist Episcopal Church.

Asbury grew up in a humble cottage, working in the local iron-works from the age of 13. The Old Mill Forge was a community in itself, a scale up from other family run cottage industries, having its own farm and chapel. Here, Asbury was introduced to an early form of Methodism, a denomination whose restrained pragmatism appealed to the stamina and resilience of the forge workers. Bible readings would introduce literacy to the lives of otherwise uned-ucated people. Even today, Methodist churches around the world are still known as 'forges'. From the age of 18, Asbury was preach-ing locally in the fields and barns around Walsall, Wednesbury and Wolverhampton, and at 22 was invited by the Methodist leader John Wesley to become an itinerant preacher. This led him to British North America, where he travelled the land by horseback, preaching in farmland, street corners, public houses, courtrooms and people's log cabin homes.

The cottage of Asbury's childhood in Great Barr still stands, dat-ing from the early 18th century, and since the 1960s becoming the museum of Bishop Asbury after sustained local suggestions. A visit also reveals how nailmakers and workers of the period lived prior to the industrial revolution, the small house being typical of the met-al-working industry, and a rare survivor from this period. The cottage is furnished simply according to the day, while additional panels tell the lost story of Bishop Francis Asbury.

Address Newton Road, Great Barr B43 6HN, +44 (0)121 556 0683, www.sandwell.gov.uk |
Getting there Bus 16 Platinum to Ray Hall Lane | Hours The Museum is open twice a year in
May and September or by appointment for group visits | Tip The site of the Old Mill Forge of
Asbury's youth is now Forge Mill Farm, an active farm and rare breeds centre, located on the
edge of Sandwell Valley Country Park (www.discoversandwell.co.uk/forge-mill-farm).

17 Black Sabbath Bench

Relax with the local heroes of heavy metal

Heavy metal has been one of Birmingham's biggest cultural exports, with Black Sabbath representing the benchmark in dark, satanic, heavy riffing. Legend has it that the genre was born when guitarist Tony Iommi created a primal, distortion-heavy style to disguise his playing limitations after losing his fingertips in an industrial accident at work. There followed 50 years of world tours, millions of album sales, and the growth of a dedicated international fan base.

Yet it is only in the last decade that the band's impact and legacy has been visibly acknowledged in the city, with Home of Metal's series of exhibitions and live events curated by Artistic Director Lisa Meyer. The band is celebrated by no fewer than five memorials on Broad Street: this bench, Black Sabbath Bridge and three pavement plaques for each of the band members (in 2023, Ozzy's own star is temporarily in storage). You can also stroll to Digbeth Coach Station for a recent, and possibly ephemeral, building-height mural of the band by graffiti artist N4T4.

The bench features four etched cut-outs of the band by artist Tarek Abdelkawi, offering an opportunity for a selfie next to your favourite band member. It is of course made entirely in metal, with portraits etched and galvanised in the Jewellery Quarter. This makes it resistant to souvenir hunters, and it now rivals the Bullring's bronze bull for the position of top selfie destination. A plaque on the bench names its creators.

Why a bench to celebrate this most dynamic of forces? Perhaps after half a century of heavy rocking, Black Sabbath have earned a rest. Furthermore, this part of Birmingham was recognised to be lacking public seating options. The bench arrived a year or two after their final live appearance, a spectacular and emotional hometown gig on 4 February, 2017. With the metal bench, the band are now permanently 'on form'.

Address Bridge over Birmingham Canal Old Line, Broad Street, Birmingham B1 | Getting there Regular bus and tram service to Brindleyplace and a short walk | Tip Compare the Sabbs' bench with the white marble forms, gently flowing water, raked gravel and cherry trees in the Zen Garden just two minutes' walk away in Oozells Square.

18 Bournville Carillon
Mechanical bells played by keyboard

This building is a gigantic musical instrument. It blends into the undeniable eccentricity of Bournville, which is known for its commitment to beautiful, liveable spaces for all. Carillons are rare anywhere, particularly in the UK, and unlike the bell towers of churches, they are played by a single performer – the carilloneur – who sits at a keyboard inside the building. Bournville Carillon was commissioned in 1906 by chocolatier George Cadbury, as a gift to workers at his factory. This followed a visit to Bruges, where he saw a particularly impressive example that would help distinguish his model village from the rest of Birmingham. It also represented part of a wider revival of the carillon, as cast bells were becoming more finely tuned, and thus more musical. With new bells being added throughout its history, this is now an epic 48-bell example.

The cubic tower upon which the carillon sits is a curious mix of subtly asymmetric Arts and Crafts style in red brick, with stone Gothic elements. Frolicking folk, carved by Benjamin Chadwick, are depicted in the panel beneath the projecting oriel window; these, and the ripe grapes on the vine decorating the keystone, may be a gentle satire on the teetotal Quaker community. Two skeletal brass clock dials remind us to *carpe diem* – seize the day – while diamond diapering in blue brick echoes the early patterns at Hay Hall (see ch. 54). The adjacent infants school has its own 'little sister' bell tower.

The carillon has regular concerts and recitals, one of which marked the death of HRH Prince Phillip, followed by 99 chimes. The bells sound twice for an hour on Saturday afternoons, usually at noon and 3pm, so time your visit and enjoy a picnic on the green opposite. As the building is also an active junior school, it's quieter during the week, sounding hourly, with single chimes on the quarter and half hours.

Address Woodbrooke Road, Bournville, Birmingham B30 1JY, www.bournvillecarillon.co.uk |
Getting there Train to Bournville, then a 13-minute walk; bus 61 or 63 to Bournville |
Hours The visitor centre on Bournville Green opposite the carillon is open Mon–Sat
10am–4.30pm | Tip From a time when clocks and sundials would offer epithets as well as
the hour, further up Linden Road, the sundial on the charming Friends Meeting House
announces 'my times are in thy hand'.

19__ The Bull

A country pub in the Gun Quarter

Despite the bull being Birmingham's most famous mascot and unofficial emblem, The Bull on Price Street on the edge of the city centre is surely Birmingham's great lost pub. With many city centre pubs closing down, becoming theme bars or acquiring a contemporary, industrial look, it's heartening to discover a pub that hasn't tried to fix what was never broken. A date on The Bull estimates c1800 as the time of construction, and the Venetian window on the first floor suggests that it was formerly a large and fashionable home.

Outside the pub is surely the world's most thoroughly informative blue plaque, which informs visitors of the pub's history, and its wider Gun Quarter setting. Inside is a cosy and welcoming atmosphere that feels much more like a country pub than an urban hostelry. To the left of the corner door is a coloured glass panel, illustrating a bull divided into what look like cuts of beef. On closer examination, the diagram gives the names of gun parts, referencing the local industry. Above the bar is a small museum's worth of ceramic jugs, with a pleasingly indiscriminate approach to selection. Elegant fine china stands beside branded corporate kitsch and 70s travel souvenirs, the whole collection evoking the phrase 'bull in a china shop'. The back room features maps and etchings of how Old Birmingham town looked in the 18th century. The pub offers a good selection of real ales, wines and spirits and has a 'winter fuel' approach to its menu.

Many discover The Bull only after living in the city for years, even though it's just a short walk from the city centre. Perhaps being just the wrong side of the ring road is the reason for the pub's relatively low profile. The focus on easing traffic speedily around the city was at the expense of a more natural pedestrian flow and economic growth, with the ring road known by many as 'the concrete collar'.

Address 1 Price Street, Birmingham B4 6JU, +44 (0)121 333 6757,
www.thebullbirmingham.co.uk | Getting there Bus 33 or 51 to Price Street | Hours Daily
noon–11pm | Tip Around the corner on Bath Street is the Gunmakers Arms, another
outlying traditional pub and home to the Two Towers Brewery (www.gunmakersarms.com).

20 __ Bullring Indoor Market
Large-scale fish retail

Before its industrial explosion, Birmingham was a quiet mediaeval market town. The Bullring markets have not moved far since first appearing in 1160 (a small sign outside humbly records the date), so perhaps it shouldn't be too surprising that the Bullring hosts the country's largest retail fish market. You might ask how this can be, given its location in deeply landlocked Birmingham. The answer lies in transport logistics: the city is a redistribution hub to supply the rest of the county, as well as savvy locals, so fish from all over the world end their journeys here.

The lower end of the Bullring Indoor Market retains an air of its mediaeval days, with hanging meat, tripe and stacked sheep heads in abundance. The air has the tang of fresh produce, and echoes with the calls of traders pursuing a deal. Enoch's butcher's stall has signs written entirely in Cantonese, welcoming and addressing the shoppers and restaurateurs of nearby Chinatown. Amongst the butchers are the fishmongers' stalls, their fresh produce laid out on ice. You'll recognise many of the popular choices, but tantalisingly there will be plenty of uncommonly encountered fish on offer, brought in from around the world, and a testament to the variety of cuisines in Birmingham.

The longest established of the stalls is Pearce's Shellfish, market traders here for five generations, and fishmongers for four of those. Over the years, Pearce's has shifted to specialising in shellfish, and no longer competes with the fresh fish stalls. This is the only place in the city where you'll find fresh oysters, and the stall is adjoined by a small bar for customers to 'eat in'. Lobster, octopus and Alaskan snow crab are usually available, and wild sea bass is a speciality with fresh samphire to go with it. Other delights include lumpfish or salmon caviar, cockles, whelks and squid ink to add to your risotto.

Address Bullring Indoor Market, Edgbaston Street, Birmingham B5 4RQ,
+44 (0)121 303 0208, www.birmingham.gov.uk/info/20150/markets | Getting there
Train to Birmingham New Street or Moor Street; buses to Bullring | Hours Mon–Sat
9am–5.30pm | Tip Stall 46 is Rohman Hardware, a densely packed cabin offering
every conceivable tool, nail, screw or electrical accessory.

21 Bullring Meteorite
A fallen star of heavy metal

Spiceal Street was the scene of a curious incident in 2000, one that few locals remember, and fewer still celebrate. It was here that a meteorite fell from the skies above the Bullring – the second time that this sizeable meteorite had fallen to earth. Rather than a huge crater, however, a commemorative plaque marks the spot and the occasion. Despite the official-looking nature of the cast metal plaque, it only serves to raise further questions: Where is the meteorite? How could it fall twice? And what is the connection with Natan, China?

The answers lie with an artwork by Cornelia Parker, titled *A Meteorite Lands in Birmingham's BullRing*. The claim about the meteorite is true: it came from a 20,000lb chunk of iron that broke up over Natan, China, in 1516. Fragments were scattered across the landscape, eventually identified and retrieved in the 1950s. Some fragments made their way to Parker, who in 2000 launched them in a firework from the roof of the Rotunda tower, as part of a celebratory display organised by Ikon Gallery. Four years later, a plaque was cast to commemorate the occasion. Unlike many plaques on buildings and benches in the city, this one invites more questions than it provides answers, and as such is particularly intriguing to visitors. It could be considered a reflection on time and space, referencing a relatively recent local artistic event, an Elizabethan (or Ming Dynasty) event on the other side of the world, and the even more remote and ancient origins of the meteor itself, before it ever struck the earth.

Parker has a similar plaque to a meteorite at Whitworth Gallery in Manchester. At floor level, few will ever notice this one; indeed, its humble design is more reminiscent of a manhole cover than a plaque or work of art. Yet, perhaps a few times a year, it nonetheless prompts an observant shopper to consider their place and role in the universe.

Address Spiceal Street, Birmingham B5 | Getting there Short walk from the city centre | Tip An identical plaque is set further round Spiceal Street, deepening the mystery for anyone who encounters it.

A METEORITE FELL
IN NATAN, CHINA IN 1516

484 YEARS LATER
ON THE NIGHT OF 26TH MARCH 2000
IT FELL FROM THE SKIES AGAIN
LANDING IN BIRMINGHAM'S BULLRING

22 Calthorpe Estate

Birmingham's garden suburb

Calthorpe Estate is a network of over a hundred Regency and Victorian streets across Edgbaston and Harborne, with a character unlike anywhere else in Birmingham. The estate began as an elegant garden suburb for upper-middle class gentlemen and merchants, and their families, taking over agricultural land and representing a clear indication of the wealth – for some – that Birmingham's industry was generating. The estate grew in stages from 1810, seeing a boom around 1880, and with more modern buildings complementing the streetscapes. Houses here are detached, classically influenced, almost uniformly whitewashed, and may variously feature iron verandas, pediments and pillars, or resemble rural Italian villas.

Many of the buildings feature coach houses and stabling, and are forward facing to demonstrate their wealth. The style is deliberately distinct from the city's default red brick, although beneath the white stucco these are all brick buildings. Unlike equivalent fashionable estates in areas such as London's Belgravia or Chelsea, these houses occupy generous plots on spacious, tree-lined boulevards. These streets invite exploration on foot, pleasingly away from traffic.

Dotted amongst the white walls are some of the city's best polychrome brick houses, and the estate does a fine line of gatehouses in High Gothic whimsy. The curious Round House on St James Road is formed around a rotundral summer house of 1818, yet on the same street is the city's leading Brutalist architect John Madin's design practice of 1957, featuring a lovely green slate screen wall cut through with lozenges. The Botanical Gardens on Westbourne Road have been a popular and rewarding destination since 1831, with 15 acres of outdoor and hothouse exotic flora. The estate's most prestigious restaurant is Simpsons on Highfield Road, celebrating British cuisine and Michelin-starred for 20 years.

Getting there Train to Five Ways or bus 23 or 24 to Calthorpe Road to arrive at the heart of Calthorpe Estate | Tip The sumptuous setting of The Edgbaston's Art Deco cocktail lounge offers an accessible taste of Calthorpe Estate's ornament and ostentation at 18 Highfield Road, Edgbaston.

23 __ Cardinal Newman Museum

'The people of Birmingham have souls too'

This small and lucid museum celebrates the life, influence and legacy of John Henry Newman, the Birmingham-based theologian, poet, thinker, cardinal and, since 2019, Saint. Newman was born in London in 1801, and became a leading academic at Oxford before settling in Birmingham in 1845 after his conversion to Catholicism. His first church was a former gin distillery in Deritend, now St Anne's Church on Alcester Street. In 1852 he moved to the current site of the Birmingham Oratory, where he remained until his death in 1890. If asked about his choice to settle here, he would wryly respond 'The people of Birmingham have souls too'.

The museum tells Newman's story through a collection of personal objects. A letter written at the age of seven shows a careful copperplate which would shame most adults. Here, too, are music scores and the handwritten verse to *The Dream of Gerontius*, later set to music by Elgar.

A display case holds a selection of possessions from Newman's study elsewhere in the house, kept intact since his death. Inside are spectacles, a razor, the wig he wore during an illness, and a tiny vial of holy water recovered from St Winefride's Well in the Welsh town of Holywell. A lamp gifted by Prime Minister William Gladstone reflects candle light to further illuminate his non-electric study. The objects are treated with a reverence befitting their transition to becoming relics, and it is clear that Newman himself was an astute collector and annotator of his own life.

Most visible in the room are the vivid red and purple cardinal's cassocks, tailored in Rome in wool and silk. Enhance your visit by booking a guided tour of the Oratory's breath-taking church and grounds, known as Birmingham's 'Little Italy'. Please see the Oratory's website for all booking details.

Address Entrance via Oratory House, 141 Hagley Road, Edgbaston, Birmingham B16 8UE, www.birminghamoratory.org.uk/cardinal-newman-museum | **Getting there** Bus 9, X 10 and 126 to Hagley Road; train to Five Ways, then a 15-minute walk | **Hours** Thu & Fri 11am–1pm, Sat 11am–3pm, Tue, Wed & Sun by appointment only | **Tip** A rare milestone placed by a 19th-century turnpike trust appears in front of Lyndon House at 62 Hagley Road, reading simply: 'To Birm 1'.

24 Castle Bromwich Gardens

Striking 18th-century formal garden

The first glimpse many people have of Castle Bromwich Hall Gardens is from a plane as they come into land at BHX. In front of the sprawling country house they see a 10-acre walled garden with a formal layout and a distinctive holly maze. They may ask 'Where's that?' But for many years, the residents of Castle Bromwich have known about the splendid survivor at the heart of their town.

In recent years the hall, which dates from 1599, has become a private hotel. It still overlooks the gardens, which have remained intact since around 1700, escaping the attentions of the English Landscape Movement, which radically re-fashioned older formal gardens. An overhaul in the 1980s rescued the gardens from decline. The years between 1680 and 1760 are celebrated, with the garden being populated with over 600 varieties of plants, trees and fruits from the period, both native and from many other countries all around the world. The only region not covered is Australasia, as trade links back then had yet to be established. But what is 'native'? A good place to ask this question is in the English apple orchard, where trees are labelled by variety, the date of their earliest mention and country of origin. What we imagine to be thoroughly English may prove to have more exotic heritage.

The gardens' original clairvoies – or sight lines – are maintained, allowing a clear view through the holly hedges, treed areas and stepped lawns to the mirror pool. An Orangery links with the Summer House, then and now used as a music room. At the lower corners of the garden, two lamias – sphinx-like creatures – guard the walls atop a pile of bones. The gardens have an active programme of live events, including music, artists' workshops, Japanese blossom picnics and family days. At harvest time you can leave with rhubarb, heritage potatoes and apples, while jams, pickles and honey are always available.

Address Chester Road, Castle Bromwich, Birmingham B36 9BT, www.castlebromwichhallgardens.org.uk | **Getting there** Bus X12 Platinum to Southfield Avenue and a five-minute walk or 94 to Heathland Avenue and a 10-minute walk | **Hours** Wed–Sun 10.30am–4.30pm | **Tip** More aeroplanes in flight at Spitfire Island, where sculptor Tim Tolkien has memorialised three spitfires soaring above the traffic, next to the factory that once made them. The sculpture is officially called *Sentinel* and can be seen most safely from B&Q car park, Dunlop Way.

25 __ Catacombs
Ancient solution to overcrowded churchyards

Catacombs are a city's solution to interring the dead when population growth means existing consecrated ground can't keep up. Underground vaults, often beneath a church, hold sealed coffins stacked several graves high. The solution dates back to ancient Rome, where the extensive catacombs were outside the city walls. Birmingham has its own catacombs on a much more modest scale in Warstone Lane Cemetery in the Jewellery Quarter. The cemetery is the 1848 solution to the need for new space for burials as Birmingham grew rapidly.

The catacombs themselves date back to 1880, occupying the site of a sandpit which provided sand for local foundries. The hollowed-out sandpit in the naturally sloping terrain allowed a more economical form of burial. The catacombs comprise three stone tiers of vaults arranged around a crescent, with each tier accessible to visitors. However, since the late 90s, the inner vaults themselves have been inaccessible. The interred are named vault by vault on stone tablets next to the ramp on the Pitsford Street side, and some plaques remain in place along the walls of the catacombs. Most came from humble backgrounds, but they are joined by the wealthy and successful typographer John Baskerville (see ch. 59).

Missing from the tranquil setting is the chapel of St Michael and All Angels, that once stood in the elevated space behind the catacombs. The chapel was badly damaged in a Second World War bombing raid, and the catacombs themselves were used as wartime air raid shelters. In recent years, the lost chapel's outline has been laid out in stone as a Garden of Memory. The official entrance is on Warstone Lane, but the catacombs are most easily accessed from Pitsford Street, with the whole cemetery rewarding the curious explorer. The ground is uneven in places, so please tread carefully amongst the tilting headstones.

Address 161–162 Warstone Lane, Birmingham B18 6NN | Getting there Train to Jewellery Quarter; bus 101 to The Clock | Hours 1 Oct–31 March 8.30am–4pm, 1 Apr–30 Sept 8.30am–7pm | Tip Head to the nearby Key Hill Cemetery (entrance on Key Hill) for another example of space-saving catacombs.

26 — Chinese Pagoda

Landmark gateway to the Chinese Quarter

The traffic island made distinct by a towering Chinese pagoda has gone by many names over the centuries. Horsefair is the earliest of these, referring to the beast market that was held here in the 18th century. On road maps it is Holloway Circus, a hollow way being a sunken track worn through the land by regular use over time. The plaque on the pagoda refers to the site as Thomas Gardens, honouring a city councillor during a 1966 subway landscaping. Since 1998, it has become known as Pagoda Island. The pagoda is in a landscaped garden with the subway entrance protected by 'foo dogs' (they actually portray lions) and a yin-yang symbol is set into the ground.

The pagoda was a gift to the city from the local Chinese supermarket chain owners Woon Wing Yip and his brother Sammy Yap, in recognition of Birmingham's support of the brothers since opening a grocery store in Digbeth in 1970. The solid stone pagoda weighs 86 tonnes, was hand-carved in Fujian, China from a local granite chosen to suit the Birmingham townscape by day, and is illuminated in different colours by night. Its eight tiers represent the luckiest number in Chinese culture, signifying wealth. The pagoda represents a gateway to the nearby Chinese Quarter, rich with restaurants, buildings that have adopted traditional designs, and with annual Lunar New Year street celebrations.

In recent years, the wider setting of the island and underpass has become rather neglected, with the extensive 1966 mosaic by Kenneth Budd now missing many sections. Between the gaps, the remaining mosaic illustrates the Horsefair's heyday, populated by traders and horses, while in the background, trams and motorcars signal the advances in technology that would spell the end of horse-powered transport. The car remains king at Pagoda Island, with recent road-widening developments to accommodate the growing volume of traffic.

Address Holloway Circus, Birmingham B1 1EG | Getting there Train to New Street, then a five-minute walk; bus 61 or 63 to Smallbrook Queensway | Tip The modest Peach Garden in Bath Passage is one of the Chinese Quarter's least visible restaurants, yet one of the most rewarding. Its backstreet setting has recently been made vibrant with graffiti art murals.

27 City Farm
A rustic sliver in an urban setting

This small plot of land just beyond the viaduct was originally a bomb site. Fearless children would explore and play here, eventually leading to the construction of an adventure playground. A solitary goat was kept on the waste land, which set the theme for the plot being a place of animal residence. City Farm has been evolving since the late-1970s, and is today a compact habitat of charming animal and vegetable encounters. It is run by St Paul's Community Development Trust, open to all and free of charge.

Visitors can explore at will, and feed the animals with corn provided by the farm. There is no agenda other than to prompt consideration of our food's origins, and the usually invisible journey from farm to fork. While children are the main visitors, the experience is meaningful for all ages. Among the hutches and enclosures are rabbits, guinea pigs, geese, turkeys and chickens. Another enclosure allows Shetland sheep to roam, and the farm's newest acquisition is two pygmy goats. Perhaps the most popular animal on the farm, however, is Homer: a sleek, white cat that prowls freely, and longs to be petted. While there are no rare species, for those who have never seen a turkey in its full feathered splendour or watched goats play fight, the visit can be a gentle revelation. The Chinese goose, with its elegant striped neck and curious, dinosaur-like head knot, is a dramatic encounter. Several planters amongst the animal enclosures are rich with fruit and vegetables, while outdoor tables and chairs allow a space to relax amongst the honks and bleats.

A diverse staff of regulars and volunteers keeps the farm running, the work giving a sense of belonging and responsibility for all involved. The rural idyll of the farm occasionally calls you back to its city setting, as freight trains rattle overhead and cars squeeze through the narrow viaduct arch opposite, their warning honks reminiscent of downtown New York.

Address Malvern Street, Balsall Heath, Birmingham B12 8NN, +44 (0)121 464 1888, www.stpaulstrust.org.uk | Getting there Bus 50 to Moseley Road Baths | Hours Mon–Fri 9.30am–4.15pm, Sat & Sun 10.30am–3.15pm | Tip Damascena Souk is an extraordinarily well-appointed deli, butcher and grocer with a Middle Eastern orientation (564 Moseley Road).

28 Coffin Works

Coffin fittings for the UK's top brass

For decades, Newman Brothers was the country's leading supplier of coffin fittings and cerements: the name plates, handles, crosses and inner soft furnishings, stopping short of supplying the coffins or caskets themselves. Opening its Fleet Street Works in 1894, Newman Brothers benefited from the opulent Victorian 'cult of death', and at its peak the company was furnishing the funerals of Winston Churchill, King George V and VI, generally meeting the requirements of the wealthier classes.

The history of the company charts the nation's downturn in extravagant expenditure. People became less willing to spend large sums of money on robust creations that would only be used once. While canny businesses adapt to the times, Newman Brothers upheld old values, not wishing to embrace plastic or adopt other cost-cutting measures. The museum is the story of these standards, and what they meant to workers and clients alike.

Visitors to the museum enter through the gift shop, punch their ticket in the old clock-in machine, then enter the works' well-preserved courtyard. Fleet Street works form an L-shape, allowing light to enter the workshops from both sides. The smell of oil and wood fills the ground floor as the old drop stamp machine is fired up to make the fittings. Moulds and dies line the walls, testament to the wealth of choice on offer. Brass plates occupy the work benches, the bigger the older.

Upstairs are the quality control and distribution rooms, where visitors can inspect the range of goods produced. The final floor is the cerements studio, a term referring to the soft furnishings of the coffin interior, as well as the shrouds and deathwear of the day. The coffin works reveals some of the practical aspects of death that are usually a mystery to us, and many people find it prompts valuable conversations on mortality that wouldn't usually arise.

Address 3–15 Fleet Street, Birmingham B3 1JP, +44 (0)121 233 4790, www.coffinworks.org | Getting there Bus 101 to Fleet Street | Hours Fri–Sun 11am–3pm | Tip Traditional and contemporary African cuisine is available next door at Bantu, with crocodile burgers a speciality (www.bantubirmingham.com).

29 Coleshill Pillory
Reminder of the ruthless days of public punishment

The pillory exemplifies the brutal approach taken in mediaeval times to public misdemeanours, measures that were still being used well into the 19th century. A wooden frame clamped around the offender's hands and head, requiring the occupant to stand and face public ridicule – and worse. The pillory was related to the more frequently seen stocks, which restricted ankles and wrists only.

The pillory at Coleshill was of a sort that combined pillory and stocks, and further incorporated a whipping post. Despite being common in most towns, this is one of just a few surviving examples left in the country. It stands an imposing 14 feet high, the renovated woodwork clearly showing the holes for two heads, two pairs of hands and the elevated cross brace on which the offenders stood. The iron brackets for shackles survive on the vertical post, but the stocks at ground level appear to have been lost over time. As functional as its design might look, the carpenter has included a subtle embellishment in the form of an acorn at the top of the structure, referencing the oak from which the sturdy pillory was made. Its former location in front of the market hall gives a clue to the more common missiles that would have been thrown by the vengeful townsfolk, but the unfortunate occupants of the pillory might also have been spat on, and pelted with stones or even dead animals. For some, the humiliation alone was enough to put a stop to further offences. For others, the pillory became a regular place of residence.

After it was used for the last time, the pillory was relocated to its present location on Church Street. Today the punishments seem barbaric, so it is perhaps a surprise to learn that they were sometimes used for minor offences that didn't warrant an appearance at a higher court, as determined by local magistrates. These might have been refusing to go to church, blasphemy, swearing, fortune telling, or as the brass plaque here notes, for drunkenness.

Address Church Hill, Coleshill B46 3AD | **Getting there** Train to Coleshill Parkway, then bus 75 A or X 13 | **Tip** Time your visit to coincide with the annual open day of Maxstoke Castle, a well-preserved, moated and fortified 14th-century manor house, which opens in June as part of the National Garden Scheme (Castle Lane, Coleshill).

30 Colley Ison Gallery

Contemporary art at the city's heart

At the heart of the Colley Ison gallery is the repertoire of like-minded artists. They share a clear love of painting, expanding on traditional techniques to create something that is always dynamic and vivid. They also have in common their association with the gallery's founder, Reuben Colley. Born in nearby Hodge Hill, Colley trained in Wolverhampton and opened the gallery in 2010 to offer a space for professional artists to exhibit their work in a well-presented setting. The 'Ison' referred to in the gallery's name is Timothy, its second director.

Colley's own paintings demonstrate an unapologetic fascination with Birmingham's urban fabric, eulogising the viaducts, pubs, overpasses and expanses of brickwork where many would see no appeal. Fortunately, plenty of others do, and there's sustained demand for this distinct aspect of the city's grainy character. Colley's work acts as a counterpoint for more flamboyant and colourful work, which often has playful or outright surreal elements. The gallery champions local, national and international contemporary original work, with a popular line of 'blue chip' art, printed in low-number editions aimed at business district clients who, in pursuit of a Hockney or Banksy, may go on to discover something unexpected.

Exhibitions at the gallery sell well, and its online business is sufficiently brisk to mean works can even sell out before a show opens. Despite being a commercial space, there's an open and welcoming atmosphere, and the gallery can be regarded as a regular cultural diversion for anyone visiting the city centre. Also significant is the ornate building the gallery occupies: this is the former Union Club of 1870, designed by Yeoville Thomason, architect of the nearby Council House. The distinctive bearded faces in stone hint at the exclusive Victorian gentlemen's club this once was.

Address 85–89 Colmore Row, Birmingham B3 2BB, +44 (0)121 236 0920, www.colleyisongallery.com | Getting there Regular buses to Colmore Row | Hours Mon–Thu 10am–6pm, Sat 10am–4pm, Sun by appointment only | Tip On Temple Row West is Damascena: Middle Eastern coffee and cuisine with a splendid interior that is both cosy and opulent; enjoy an excellent view over Cathedral Square from the huge front window (www.damascena.co.uk).

31 The Conservatoire

An urban castle of concerts

The Royal Birmingham Conservatoire is a new, purpose-built music and acting college, located in Birmingham City University's City Centre campus in Eastside. While the building is new, the Conservatoire as a school for music has been around since 1859, originally part of the Birmingham and Midland Institute, and more recently merging with Birmingham School of Acting. Opening in 2018 after being granted a royal title by Queen Elizabeth II, the college is very much a public building, and welcomes music-lovers to enjoy regular recitals, concerts, talks and events.

Approaching the Conservatoire has the feel of encountering a castle, which was expressly the intention of architects Feilden Clegg Bradley Studios. Directly beside the college is the busy A 47, and the sheer rises of the building's bold exterior effectively shield the sounds within from those without. Inside, the scale is similarly epic, the foyer being spread over three levels. The interior is rich with wood, giving the space a warm and welcoming feel. At the heart of the Conservatoire is the 500-seat concert hall, a timber-lined auditorium with state-of-the-art acoustic baffles. The rhythm and pattern here is all about sound excellence but it has an extraordinary visual impact too. There is a more modest recital hall, an experimental space known as the black box, and a separate space for Eastside Jazz Club.

The ground floor has a café, while the upper levels contain the college elements: recording studios, classrooms and practice spaces. The Conservatoire's music programme is a mix of classical, contemporary composition, opera, choral and more experimental performances. Postgraduate performers regularly appear on the bill. There are regular talks on music, and while some lunchtime recitals are free, they are often fully booked before the performance, so be sure to plan ahead.

Address 200 Jennens Road, Birmingham B4 7XR, +44 (0)121 331 5901, www.bcu.ac.uk/
conservatoire | Getting there Bus 94 to Millennium Point | Tip Accessible from Gopsal
Street is BCU's Student Union Bar in the Curzon Building, which sympathetically
incorporates the Eagle and Ball pub, dating from around 1840.

32 Cornwall Street

Unique Metropolitan Arts and Crafts townhouses

You are unlikely to visit Cornwall Street unless you're an art student or attending a lecture at the Birmingham Midland Institute, but on the street's upper section are six Victorian and Edwardian townhouses unlike anything else in the city – or indeed the country.

These buildings were four-storey medical and dentistry practices, with residential rooms upstairs and the surgery and consulting rooms downstairs. Each block is very different to its neighbour. Arts and Crafts tradition is subtler than the rather intense Victorian neo-classical tradition, and the townhouses of Cornwall Street are each styled with charm, wit, a degree of asymmetry, and a keen appreciation of local materials: in Birmingham that means red brick, terracotta, stone and wrought ironwork, rather than the whitewashed regency of London.

While Birmingham has its own district with London pretensions (see ch. 22), Cornwall Street represents a more authentic response to the fabric of the second city. From left to right – not the order in which they were built – the architectural stylings become more ambitious, as if attracting the attention of their elegant, opulent neighbour, the School of Art. The pink and white accents of numbers 89 and 91 must have raised some eyebrows when they appeared in 1905, and were surely influenced by the nearby Eagle Insurance building, with its playful checkerboard parapet (see ch. 38). Meanwhile, number 85 seems to have more storeys than number 87 in the same block, the imbalance being key to the Arts and Crafts style.

The remainder of Cornwall Street maintains a harmonious townscape not usually seen in Birmingham: buildings sprout turrets, weathervanes and moulded enrichments, with even recent buildings using the same terracotta hues and materials in their design – an acknowledgment of the tradition of care once prevalent in the city.

Address 85–93 Cornwall Street, Birmingham B3 3BY | Getting there Short walk from the city centre | Tip The palatial Birmingham School of Art at 6 Margaret Street is open to the public during the Fine Art students' final shows in summer (www.bcu.ac.uk/about-us).

33 Dayus Square
Home of The Girl from Hockley

There is a cluster of interesting features in Dayus Square, including some it would be possible to miss. The square takes its name from Kathleen Dayus, born in Hockley in 1903, and who in her later years chronicled her experiences of growing up in nearby Camden Drive. Her detailed accounts of a life of arduous work and grinding poverty in a working class family became best-sellers, and she was awarded an honorary degree by the University of Birmingham for her writing, as the lives of the workers who kept Birmingham's economy running were rarely chronicled first-hand. Dayus died in 2003, aged 99.

On the north side of the square, a small bronze sculpture at ground level takes the form of two curling pages from Dayus' books. A splendid ghost sign occupies the upper reaches of a handsome Georgian house at 106 Albion Street. Jones and Palmer were a 'printers and stationers (etc etc)', and their sign is still vivid decades later. The bricks are used as a guide to the layout, and you can just see a pale blue drop shadow, used to give the letters a 3-D appearance. The Jewellery Quarter has many other such faded memories of the past.

The courtyard behind the printers contains a row of 'three-quarter houses', a humble living option in 1840, but superior to the back-to-back arrangements found across the city, such as those still standing on Inge Street. Less missable in Dayus Square is the cheerful pub, once the George and Dragon, now the Pig and Tail, converted from a Georgian house into a comprehensively glazed bar room in 1875. It stood as a gloomy ruin for decades, but is now active once more. At the east end of the square is the former Fire Station, built in bright red brick and bearing the city's Forward motto in a crest. The station is topped with a decorative cupola, and a fire watch tower left over from the Second World War.

Address Dayus Square, Birmingham B1 3ED | Getting there Bus 101 to Graham Street |
Tip Heaton House on Camden Street is an attractive villa of the early 19th century. Once a
gentleman's domestic residence set in formal gardens, the house was gradually swallowed up
by factories on all sides until 2020, when it emerged, slightly scarred, from its industrial prison.

34 Dhamma Talaka Pagoda
The Reservoir of Truth in the heart of Ladywood

A trio of intriguing towers spikes the skyline around Edgbaston Reservoir (see ch. 39). Most visible are the Waterworks Tower and Perrott's Folly (see ch. 86) but even more astonishing is the shining golden stupa of the Dhamma Talaka Peace Pagoda, which since 1998 has piqued curiosity from viewers circumnavigating the reservoir. Appropriately for the location, its name translates as 'the reservoir of truth' and this is the only instance of a Burmese traditional temple appearing anywhere in the western hemisphere. If you are prompted to ask 'Why Birmingham?', one answer is that the city is rich with diverse temples, synagogues, mosques and churches, and offers the ideal spiritual landscape for this temple.

The greater pagoda complex includes the Rewata Dhamma Buddhist academy and the Sangharama Monastery: the robed monks can regularly be seen walking around the circumference of the reservoir. The pagoda is set in a small garden with rose bushes and a koi carp pool. Statues of traditional white and gold lions flank the entrance to the temple, which has doors made from intricately carved teak. The pagoda is a rewarding encounter if seen from the reservoir or from Osler Street, but is also open to the public. It welcomes visitors by advance appointment, including worshippers of all faiths, or indeed of none. Meditation courses are also available for those seeking peace.

Inside, a spectacular shrine is populated by statues of the Buddha, ornate parasols, burning incense and freshly cut flowers arranged around a golden throne. A domed ceiling is decorated by moulded reliefs made by the Myanmar artist U Win Tin, depicting 'The Twenty Eight Buddhas'. Opulent rugs and richly upholstered chairs further furnish the single round room. Encountering this serene and sacred inner space set in an already tranquil natural landscape is a poignant and memorable experience.

Address 29/31 Osler Street, Birmingham B16 9EU, +44 (0)121 454 6591, www.birminghambuddhistvihara.org | Getting there Open to the public by appointment | Hours Regular buses to Hagley Road, then a 10-minute walk | Tip The Birmingham Canal Old Line, accessible from the bottom of Osler Street, offers a tranquil walking route back to the city centre.

35__The Diskery

Record shop that became a museum of itself

The Diskery is an old-fashioned record shop selling what may be known to successive generations as records, albums, LPs, vinyl or – in the recent comeback years – as 'vinyls'. Record shops have been increasingly absent from the high street since the 2000s, so to encounter an active and vibrant shop, jam-packed with racks of records, feels like either an entirely new and bewildering experience to a new generation of music fans, or a time-travel moment to those who remember and love them. After decades of resolutely weathering the many changes in how music is made, played and consumed, the shop has become a 'museum of itself'. Only Spillers in Cardiff is older in the UK.

The Diskery was opened in 1952 by Morris Hunting as an outlet for jazz and swing, relocating a couple of times before settling in Bromsgrove Street in 1972. Morris ran the shop until his death in 2012, when it was taken over by current owner Lee Dearn, alongside old hand Liam Scully, who has been with the shop since 1972. It occupies a former house of 1792, creaking at the seams with the wealth of records within. A visit to the Diskery represents everything that isn't included in a digital download: LP sleeves, picture disks, CDs, posters, music memorabilia in racks, boxes and even stapled to the ceiling. The shop features a listening booth that allows customers to listen to disks before buying them.

Regulars visit for the atmosphere as much as to browse, crate diggers come in search of samples, and families bring a new generation of music-lovers, amazed at the antique music formats. In recent years, the shop has also managed to squeeze in live gigs and DJs. In 2015, The Diskery lent shelves of records to Ikon Gallery to help recreate the home of prominent British Jamaican photographer Vanley Burke. The Ikon's shop features a rack of albums from The Diskery as a permanent fixture.

Address 99 Bromsgrove Street, Birmingham B5 6QB, +44 (0)121 622 2219,
www.thediskery.net | Getting there Bus 61 or 63 to Wrentham Street | Tip Across the
ring road on Irving Street lies the distinctive discoid church of St Catherine of Siena.

36 Duddeston Viaduct

The folly of early railway rivalry

Despite being the largest structure in this guidebook, it is easy to overlook Duddeston Viaduct, or rather to overlook its significance. Digbeth is characterised by its colossal blue brick viaduct arches, two lines of which vault rhythmically for half a mile over the streets and industries below. Trains regularly rumble towards Moor Street Station, but nothing travels along the Duddeston line. Indeed, nothing ever has, as no tracks were ever laid. This is the story of early competing railway companies, mergers, and stubbornness in the face of the huge amounts of money available as railways overtook waterways as a means of travel and freight.

In 1846, London & North Western and Midland Railway thwarted their rival Great Western Railway's access to their intended destination stations, and GWR instead built Snow Hill station and tunnel at monumental cost. Meanwhile, Great Western Railway abandoned their elevated track where it stood unfinished. Over the years, the empty spur has been used as a shunting yard, an unloading area for rural cattle heading to Bullring Market, and has inspired generations of architects in imaginative but unrealised visions of the elevated space. Walking alongside it through Digbeth you get a sense of the flora growing up there, with Google Maps' satellite view revealing the full extent of the wild growth. Every few years, the woodland is cleared away to avoid the roots damaging the structure and causing chaos below.

At Liverpool Street the line breaks for the road, leaving a wedge-shaped island between Liverpool Street and Great Barr Street. Anyone who has visited New York may be reminded of the High Line, a popular public park and greenway occupying a former one-and-a-half mile section of former railway. The arrival of HS2 in 2026 is certain to prompt thoughts about Digbeth's railway heritage, and the long dreamt-of Sky Park may yet emerge as a reality.

Address Starts on Upper Trinity Street, Birmingham B9 4EG, ends on Montague Street, Birmingham B5 5SE | Getting there Bus 3 or 4 to Adderley Street | Tip Follow the spiral path up a man-made mound in Kingston Hill Local Park to discover a standing stone sculpture with a good view of the city's skyline (Kingston Road).

37__Duran Duran House

Deco lodge was pop group's early practice room

'Detached riverside cottage with chic Art Deco flair' is how a late-70s estate agent might have described the house where Duran Duran rehearsed, and where one early member resided.

Birmingham's industrial buildings often show a subtle design flair to mark owners' pride in their company. The compact 1930s building was probably a caretaker's lodge connected with the nearby factory, and shows the gently streamlined domestic design sensibilities of the day. One side is distinctly on a diagonal, as it leans into the course of the river Rea flowing below the bridge, while at the back, there's a small garden space, now overgrown.

Low-rent industrial spaces are popular with artists and bands who need non-residential spaces to spread out and make noise. This particular house was home for Duran Duran's short-term lead singer and songwriter Andy Wickett, and also became a convenient rehearsal space for local bands and a late night destination after clubbing at Barbarella's. Despite some major label interest, Wickett left the band in 1979, but mentored his replacement, Simon Le Bon, with singing lessons, as the band continued to rehearse there. Two of Wickett's songs went on to become hits: 'Girls on Film' was written while on the nightshift at Cadbury's chocolate factory, and is it possible that 'Rio', about the mighty Rio Grande river in Mexico, was born from imagining a more impressive water course than the feeble trickle beneath Cheapside?

Today, the house maintains a certain timeless panache, but it hasn't been inhabited for some time: a faded *Gladiators* VHS sits on the mantelpiece in the living room downstairs, and the door has been graffitied 'Taylor B9', echoing the three Duran Duran members who share this surname. While the building has no outward clues to its musical heritage, it is nonetheless tagged 'Duran Duran spiritual home' on Google Maps.

Address 260 Cheapside, Deritend, Birmingham B5 6AY | Getting there Bus 50 to
Bradford Street | Tip Duranies should head next to Rum Runner Yard, off Regency Wharf
where a blue plaque mounted on a balcony celebrates the site of the Rum Runner nightclub.
The band regularly performed live here in 1979 and 1980.

38 Eagle Insurance Building

The 20th century starts here

Eagle Insurance is a handsome building that you may turn to admire as you head towards Victoria Square, or perhaps as you pop inside for a coffee. The city centre contains many fine examples of commercial architecture but for architectural historians, this building ranks alongside such heavyweights as St Philip's Cathedral and the Town Hall.

Eagle Insurance is important as it marks a transition between the Arts and Crafts and Moderne styles – decorative, but tastefully restrained. This was architect William Lethaby's only urban building, with homes and churches being his usual focus. He was deeply interested in the symbolic meaning of ornament in architecture, rejecting the showy designs seen on many other Victorian buildings of the time. Every element on the building's facade has meaning. The chessboard parapet is a skyscape framing the eagle coming in to land, with several suns occupying the heavens under a rolling cloud line. The sun motif appears again lower down in the two bronze doors, and even the modern building opposite reflects some of these solar disks. These doorways are faced in black limestone, swimming with fossils and topped by arches borrowed from Buddhist temples. The windows are far more generous than others of the time, being the entire height of that storey, and making the ground floor more about glass than stone. The treatment of daylight as a commodity was a recurring theme of 20th century architecture, and grew popular in the years after Lethaby introduced it.

The building uses modern materials in its construction and the concrete floors and grid of steel joists is celebrated and visible in the design – another enduring modern tradition. Lethaby was to design only one more building after this, then focussed on writing, ever trying to fine-tune his symbolist theories. Eagle Insurance bears the date 1900, proudly heralding a new age in architecture.

Address 124 Colmore Row, Birmingham B3 3SD | Getting there Train to New Street, then a six-minute walk; various buses to Colmore Row | Tip More symbolic stone birds can be found at 79–83 Colmore Row, at the silversmith William Spurrier's showroom of 1873. Four slender cranes bury their heads into the stone brackets above them, and the building expresses their collective dream.

39 _Edgbaston Reservoir

Birmingham-on-Sea

When the reservoir opened in 1829, no one considered either canals or reservoirs as leisure destinations: they were about the hard work of transporting heavy goods and keeping them afloat. Since the decline of heavy industry, however, people now view the waterways as tranquil environments away from busy city life. Following the canals in Birmingham may well lead you to Edgbaston Reservoir, which serves to keep the canals topped up and functioning (the city's drinking water is channeled in especially from Wales, see ch. 41).

Since 1957, Edgbaston Reservoir has been a corporation park – one with an unusually impressive duck pond. The land surrounding the water is ideal for walking, running or cycling, and features outdoor gym equipment along the way. It is a haven for water birds, newts, bats and other wildlife. From its western shore, the reservoir becomes an infinity pool, with the city's skyline dropping below the watery horizon. The water is the obvious attraction, and at nearly three kilometres in circumference this is the nearest you'll get to a coastal stroll in Birmingham. On the way round you'll see evidence of activity by the yacht club, the rowing club and anglers. The hidden currents of the draining water and the icy temperatures mean swimming is out of the question, however.

In recent years, July has become the date for the Nowka Bais festival, the traditional Bangladeshi dragon boat racing celebrations that follow the Monsoon in rural villages, which is accompanied by music, dancing and street food. Perhaps the reservoir's most notable historic event was the 1873 tightrope crossing by French funambulist Charles Blondin, in front of a crowd of thousands. Not finding a local waterfall or ravine, the scale of the reservoir offered a suitable challenge. The sheer distance meant that even his longest, strongest cable dipped beneath the surface of the water at the half-way point.

Address 115 Reservoir Road, Ladywood, Birmingham B16 9EE, www.birmingham.gov.uk/reservoir | Getting there 20-minute walk from the city centre; bus 82 or 87 to Heath Street, then a 12-minute walk | Tip The tightrope crossing is celebrated by a sculpture of Blondin in full armour and plumage headdress on Ladywood Middleway, opposite St Vincent Street West.

40 Edith Holden Country
Nature walks of an Edwardian lady

The surprise best-seller of 1977 was *The Country Diary of an Edwardian Lady*, the nature notes made during 1906 by school teacher and artist Edith Holden. The book sold over a million copies that year, and was given a further boost in 1984 with a TV drama. The journal contained painted illustrations, handwritten poetry, musings and observations on the seasons and local wildlife, and was never intended to be seen by more than a few close friends and family.

The success was at least partially down to a widespread reflection on the close relationship with nature that had been lost in just 70 years, and it was quite common for girls and young women to keep such a journal. For some, the surprise was that the nature rambles took place in Birmingham and neighbouring Solihull. More than a century later, many of the places visited by Holden on her rural walks and bike rides remain intact, and are attractive destinations. The places mentioned in the diary form a loose line running from what is now the airport in the north to Henley-in-Arden in the south, including Knowle, Elmdon Park, Widney, Bentley Heath and Packwood House. Two regular destinations – Baddesley Clinton and Temple Balsall – are linked by the Heart of England Way, which allows a road-free countryside walk. The exact routes taken by Holden are unknown, but the meadows, woodlands, flora and fauna they contain resemble the countryside she recorded, allowing a creative and exploratory interpretation of where she may have walked.

Holden's diary was intended as a model for her art students to follow, and she later found success as a nature illustrator. The Holden family were keen spiritualists and regularly received and recorded messages from the spirit world. However, Edith died in tragic circumstances aged 48, drowning in the River Thames near Kew Gardens while reaching for a branch of chestnut buds.

Address Join the Heart of England Way at the moated manor house of Baddesley Clinton, Rising Lane, Knowle, Solihull B93 0DQ, +44 (0)1564 783294, www.nationaltrust.org.uk/ baddesley-clinton | Getting there Train to Lapworth, then a 30-minute walk | Hours Daily 9am–5pm | Tip Packwood House is another rural National Trust property visited by Edith on Packwood Lane, Solihull – take the train to Dorridge, then a 40-minute walk.

41 Elan Valley Model

Tribute to Birmingham's drinking water source

It is easy to take these things for granted. The Elan Valley Water-works model in Cannon Hill Park offers a subtle eulogy from 1961 to the Victorian corporation's care for its citizens. As a highly industrialised city whose residents often lived in close proximity, mortal diseases could be prevented by having access to clean water. In order to supply clean, safe drinking water to the Birmingham population, a 72-mile aqueduct was constructed from mid-Wales into the heart of the city. Through gravity alone, over the course of several days the water flows from the picturesque Elan valley, to ultimately emerge from Birmingham taps.

This feat of engineering is as simple in concept as it is bold in construction, and exemplifies the scale of endeavour at which the Victorians operated. The ambitious scheme may have been influenced by the construction of the canals throughout the city, but ultimately the idea is borrowed from the Ancient Romans. The model itself works as a fountain as well as an educational prompt, with steep grassy contours defining the valley, accented by rocky outcrops, and with shrubs representing hillside forests. Concrete dams occupy the upper reaches of the valley, while downstream it is populated with the tiny buildings of the village of Elan: a model village in two senses. Elan has another Birmingham connection: it was designed by Herbert Tudor Buckland, an Arts and Crafts architect who lived in Edgbaston.

The walls that surround the model are made from recycled corporation kerbstones. The pools are visited by water birds from the park, including moorhens, ducks, and even the occasional heron. There has been some wear over the last 60 years: one miniature concrete valve tower is missing, and indeed, the water itself does not always flow. Another sculptural response to the city's water sources appears on Laura Potter's *Findings Trail* (see ch. 46).

Address Cannon Hill Park, Russell Road, Moseley, Birmingham B13 8RD | Getting there Bus 35 to Edgbaston Road; cycle along National Cycle Route 5 from Suffolk Street Queensway | Hours Cannon Hill Park is open 7.30am–dusk | Tip Another Welsh water connection sits by the boating lake outside Midland Arts Centre: a large boulder, sometimes called 'The Meteor', is actually a glacial erratic, having arrived here on the back of a glacier sometime during the last Ice Age.

42 The Emergence of Women
Side-lined tapestry chronicles women's history

A walk through the International Convention Centre shows that it is well furnished with art in a variety of styles and materials. Alexander Beleschenko's colourful glasswork, Vincent Woropay's chrome-plated tribute to construction techniques, Richard Perry's fertile wood carvings and Roderick Tye's cast bronze cloud are all valuable additions to the city's public art repertoire. Mounted on a wall to the right of the entrance from Centenary Square and looking rather marginalised next to the boys' work is the ambitious multi-panel tapestry *Depicting the Emergence of Women in the 20th Century*, created by the Townswomen's Guild.

This appliqué and embroidered polyptych was overseen by Marion Beattie, and illustrates many historically significant moments and firsts from women's history. The central panel depicts a TG meeting in progress, flanked by eight panels from the junior members of the guild, that convey their individual interests. Amongst the outer 24 embroidered panels is pioneer aviator Amy Johnson, depicted with her trusty biplane, Jason. Shown at the 1986 Commonwealth Games is heptathlon gold medallist Judy Simpson. The horse rider is Princess Anne, the first royal to compete in the Olympic Games. The yacht celebrates Clare Francis, the first woman to sail the Atlantic. The cosmonaut panel honours Valentina Tereshkova, the first woman in space (the red planet landscape hints at a future first). Scattered amongst these are the various emblems, logos and coats of arms associated with the TG over the years. Other panels depict professional successes in engineering, fashion, politics and the armed services.

Is it actually a tapestry? Although that process is closer to weaving than embroidery, a large assembly of textiles depicting scenes has over time become known as such, the Bayeux Tapestry being the best known example of this looser naming.

Address The ICC, 8 Centenary Square, Birmingham B1 2EA | Getting there Bus or tram to Broad Street | Hours Daily 7am–11pm | Tip A plaque in the Round Room of Birmingham Museum and Art Gallery acknowledges the principles – but not the actions – of the suffragette Bertha Ryland, who in 1914 slashed a painting there as part of a campaign to allow votes for women.

43 __ The Face of the Moon
John Russell's lunar landscape in pastel

It looks like a photograph, but John Russell's pastel portrait of the moon was hand-drawn sometime in the late 18th century. It is, however, rendered with an intense accuracy and by scientific means: Russell drew what he saw of the moon through his telescope. It is a loving tribute, as considered as the portraits he would usually capture.

The work hangs above the fireplace in Matthew Boulton's study at Soho House. For Boulton, the moon represented a practical solution for scheduling the gatherings of his dinner club for the scientists, manufacturers, writers and thinkers of Birmingham and beyond. By meeting on the night of the full moon, give or take a day, he could offer a better chance of night-time illumination for his guests, at a time before street lighting had been invented. The moon gave its name to the Lunar Circle, later the Lunar Society, and became an enduring emblem for the 'Lunaticks' as the members styled themselves. Bolton planned to install an observatory at Soho House, and while that never happened, he would spend evenings on the roof peering through his telescope at various heavenly bodies.

Russell's study draws you in, its craters, seas and curious shapes having hypnotic allure. It may at first seem to be presented in black and white, but a closer look at the shadows of pastel – Russell's usual medium – shows a subtle use of colour: amongst the dark seas are various hues of green, blue and ochre. The night sky in which it hangs is not quite black, but an exceptionally deep blue. By capturing the moon in its waxing gibbous phase rather than full, as Boulton might have preferred, Russell allows us to see the lunar surface texture at the point where the sunlight reaches the shadow. As Boulton and other members of the Lunar Society would have understood, without an atmosphere to protect it, the moon is deeply scarred by meteorites.

Address Soho House, Soho Avenue, Birmingham B18 5LB, +44 (0)121 348 8150, www.birminghammuseums.org.uk/soho | **Getting there** Bus 74 to Rose Hill Road | **Tip** An accurate and elaborately labelled lunar globe sits on Boulton's desk, where others might have a terrestrial globe.

44_ Fellows, Morton & Clayton

Ark-shaped HQ for the mighty canal carriers

At the heart of Birmingham's industry was its network of canals, having no river or port to otherwise facilitate shipping. Fellows, Morton and Clayton, which once occupied the huge boat shed on Fazeley Street, was the main carrying fleet in the country. The company's proud sign built into the windowless brick facade communicates the firm's scale and permanence.

The 3-D interlocking blocks, in moulded, glazed terracotta, show a typographer's touch in the kerns. The sign doesn't mention 'boat builders', even though that was the principal function of this giant shed. The year 1935 appears in the upper reaches, when the company was at the height of its powers and approaching its centenary. But beware of dates on buildings, as they may mean several things: the company itself dates back to 1837, and was around long enough to see the transition from horse boats to steamers to motorboats – all of which it built. The company had its own trademark style of sleek, graceful vessels constructed from riveted iron and nicknamed 'Joshers' after Joshua Fellows, one of the company's three directors. Perhaps anticipating a decline in freight transport on the canals in the face of mass road transport, it went into voluntary liquidation in 1947.

The building is worth seeing from the canal, as many would have originally approached it. Join the canal further up Fazeley Street, drop down onto the Digbeth Branch Canal, then turn left onto the Grand Union Canal. From here, you can see that the building resembles an oil tanker, or maybe even Noah's Ark. What may seem to be a playful architectural reference to boat building is in fact coincidental; indeed, the prow of the 'boat' does not curve symmetrically. The shape is entirely a product of economical use of industrial land, and is actually a winding hole to allow narrowboats to turn in the canal or into the boatyard.

Address 122 Fazeley Street, Birmingham B5 5RS | Getting there Train or bus to Moor Street, then a 10-minute walk | Tip Offering everything from perfumery and stationery to leather goods and fireworks, Latifs family-owned discount department store, with the motto 'Stack them high and let it fly', has been trading in Digbeth since 1956, and recently relocated to Pickford Street (www.latifs.co.uk).

45 Fertility Seats

Public benches allow a pregnant pause

Victoria Square saw a comprehensive re-design in 1993, which introduced several enduringly popular public art works. The design was that of Rory Coonan, Director of Architecture at the Arts Council of Great Britain and responsible for its public art programme. Funding for the project came from the City Council and the European Union.

Coonan's idea was to create a *gesamkunstwerk* or 'total work of art', commissioning artists and craftspeople to decorate a new pedestrian square on two levels and banishing motor vehicles from its extent. The symmetrical layout included *The Guardians*, a pair of sphinxes by Indian sculptor Dhruva Mistry. Male and female, they loaf either side of the Square's flowing staircases. A boy and girl kneel in the lower pool in a work entitled *Youth*. A bronze figure called *River* in the top pool attracted the *soubriquet* 'Floozie in the Jacuzzi' and salmon, seahorses and platonic solids appear whenever the pool is empty.

Lines from T S Eliot's *Four Quartets* were incised around the edge of the pool, which is a geometrical superellipse drawn by P V Coonan, Rory's father. The lettering is by Bettina Furnée of the Kindersley workshop.

A theme of life energy and fecundity runs through the whole design, notably in the details of the blue metal benches which populate the square. Cut into the backs are the distinctive silhouettes of spermatozoa, fertilising an egg at the centre of the bench. Children are most likely to notice the numerous trios of spinning bronze balls set into the nearby railings. On closer examination, the rotating spheres are the swimming heads of many wriggling forms, their flagella extending downwards and their trajectory heading up towards an ovum. Seen from above, the layout of the fountain resembles a uterus, the lines and ripples of the life force radiating from it in coloured bands of paving stones.

Address Waterloo Street, Birmingham B2 5TJ. The benches may be repositioned elsewhere in the square during the Frankfurt Christmas Market. | **Getting there** Train to New Street, then a five-minute walk; buses to Colmore Row | **Tip** Between Victoria Square and the Town Hall are the city's imperial measurements: brass plaques set into granite and arranged to give accurate distances of links, feet, metres, poles and dekametres as once determined by the Standards Department of the Board of Trade and provided for public use.

46 Findings Trail

Lost and found moments from past and present

On your first encounter with the *Findings Trail* you might think you've spotted a lost mobile phone on the ground, or be perplexed by the presence of two kitchen taps emerging from the pavement. On closer inspection, however, these mystery objects turn out to be bronze casts of items and emblems relating to the past and present of the immediate vicinity.

If you walk the route regularly, you'll discover that what you had perhaps taken to be access points or manhole covers turn out to be a sequence of plaques set into the pavement, and lettered A-Z for your convenience. Installed in 1999 along Newhall Street and Graham Street, the trail illustrates a route from the city centre into the Jewellery Quarter. Artist Laura Potter responded to Mick Thacker and Mark Renn's nearby *Charm Bracelet Trail*, but determined to use more poetic and even mysterious allusions rather than their straight heritage readings. Accompanied by an explanatory leaflet upon its launch, the work now requires more involved consideration. Of note is the fact that while the trail was originally intended to be in place for 10 years, it is still largely intact two decades later. Don't spend too long looking for 'S', which fell victim to roadworks a few years ago.

Many plaques are straightforward in their meaning, such as the phone handset at Telephone House, while others are rather more subtle: the kitchen taps are captioned 'Water from the Welsh mountains' which refers to the aqueduct that conveys drinking water to the city (see ch.41). Indeed, the building here used to be the headquarters for Severn Trent Water. Several elements of the trail are also in out-of-the-way places to avoid being trip hazards, and bring a distinct transformative magic to areas of the city where art may be least expected. Becoming aware of the trail attunes the senses for other discoveries across the city.

Address Along Newhall Street and Graham Street, beginning at the junction with Lionel Street | Getting there Short walk from the city centre | Tip Follow the *Charm Bracelet Trail* deeper into the Jewellery Quarter, which picks up from where the *Findings Trail* U-turns at Frederick Street.

47__Foka Wolf

Rising star of savage street art

Popping up all over the city are Foka Wolf's paste-ups: bold graphics, surreal ideas and satirical interventions that leave those who spot them wondering exactly what they are. Early interventions were handmade notices such as the gold-trimmed advert for 'Louie Vutton' handbags ('real and good') placed on a lamppost outside the Louis Vuitton shop. These evolved into larger-scale printed multiples of fake adverts, promoting voodoo classes for kids, how to adopt a hyena, and where to skill up as a moped mugger. A recurring theme is sending up corporate greed.

The adverts are pitched a fair few strides beyond credibility, but their unexpected context in the public domain always manages to catch some people out. The audience is greatly extended by speedily shared coverage on social media. Fact-checking website service Snopes had to step in to explain that Conservative Party posters on the London Underground promising to 'cut all homeless people in half by 2025' were in fact a joke. A gentler side to Foka Wolf's street art is the signature bony thumbs-up graphic, and the overnight appearance of a towering Pat Butcher, familiar to *Eastenders* viewers of yesteryear.

Foka Wolf operates anonymously to cover his or her tracks, and arrives masked to rare public appearances. Larger works may even be a group effort by loyal supporters. Away from the street, Foka Wolf's website shop reveals a graphic design background and fine art leanings, still with the same prankster outlook, such as the 'exit reality' LED lightbox sculpture or the boxed 'key to another dimension'. Exhibitions pre-empt the next wave of chaos before it hits the streets. How best to catch the artist's work? The nature of the paste up means it may not last very long so keep an eye on Foka Wolf's social media accounts to find current examples. Once you recognise the style, you will start seeing it everywhere.

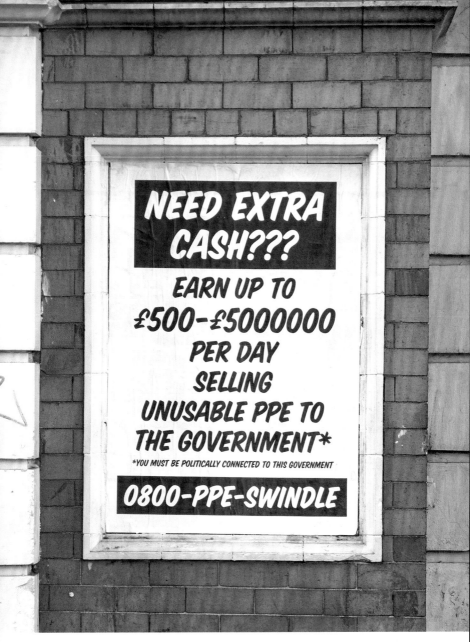

Address Rea Studios at 90 Floodgate Street, Deritend, Birmingham B5 5SS features the mighty mural of the non-existent Birmingham Screwdriver Company; www.megacorpglobal.com; Instagram and Twitter @fokawolf | Getting there Buses to Deritend, then a five-minute walk | Tip Floodgate Street is also the unofficial permanent gallery space for the street art and graffiti murals of Gent 48, whose colourful and intense characters populate several walls here.

48__Galton Bridge
Mighty ironwork spans a man-made valley

Galton Bridge is impressive cast iron lattice-work engineering from a time when the race was on to build bridges ever stronger and longer, while maintaining their elegance. It was named after the noted Birmingham gunsmith and Quaker, Samuel Galton Jr, who also owned the land. The bridge appeared in the later days of the Industrial Revolution, and features road, canal and (some years later) rail. It is one of Thomas Telford's later bridge designs, and when it opened in 1829 it was the longest single-span bridge in the world, measuring 151 feet. It is now a Grade I listed structure.

The bridge can be accessed from the curious split-level Smethwick Galton Bridge railway station (its tracks overlap in different directions), 10 minutes' journey from New Street Station. Turn left from the station to access Galton Bridge at surface level. For many years the bridge carried the traffic of Roebuck Lane across, but has been pedestrian since 1975, when traffic was considered too heavy for the bridge to support. This vantage allows you to gawk at the chasm below, containing rail and canal in a gorge which is conspicuously sunken for the region's otherwise flat landscape. This is because Galton Valley is an 'earthworks': the entire valley was created at the same time as the bridge, replacing the time-consuming flight of locks which previously straddled the landscape.

The scale of the bridge is best appreciated from below, so cross the bridge and follow the curving ramp down to the towpath of the New Main Line canal. Nearly 200 years later, it still creates a dramatic impression, balanced 60 feet above the canal and would have been much admired at the time for its lightness and economy of material. The bridge was cast in six sections at the Horseley Ironworks in Tipton, a foundry specialising in canal bridges. The foundry's name is hidden in several discreet places around Galton Bridge, which also proudly bears its name for the benefit of passing canal navigators.

Address Roebuck Lane, Smethwick B66 1BS | **Getting there** Train to Galton Bridge or bus 87 Platinum to Smethwick Galton Bridge Station | **Tip** Bridging the parallel Birmingham Canal is the earlier Summit Bridge, made entirely of brick and representing a comparable lock-reduction measure of 1799.

49 Grand Union Gallery

Cutting edge art at the old blade works

The 'Grand Union' of the gallery's name comes from the nearby canal linking Birmingham to London, but it could also stand for the ambitious bringing together of artists, curators and the public into a single space. The vision in 2010 by the group founding artists and curators, including current Director Cheryl Jones, was to combine much-needed studio space with a gallery space exhibiting new work by UK and international artists, who would create pieces specifically for the space, and give local emerging curators a place to refine their craft.

Grand Union occupies units in Minerva Works that were once industrial blade smiths: just press the buzzer for entry. Since Grand Union arrived, Minerva Works has become known as a creative destination as much as for industrial use, with several established galleries and performance spaces opening there, including Centrala, Vivid Projects and Stryx. The gallery is at the centre of the Grand Union experience, but they also have community-embedded projects popping up around the city. Recently, The Growing Project has nurtured edibles in green spaces tended by the residents of local hostels, and the gallery now has its own herb garden by the canal.

In 2021, Programme Director Kim McAleese was on the panel of judges for that year's Turner Prize, and ambitious future plans involve relocating to the huge Junction Works building round the corner. The creatively unifying nature of Grand Union can also be seen during the monthly First Friday events, taking place on (naturally) the first Friday of every month. In 2014, an alliance of local arts spaces – Grand Union, Eastside Projects and Friction Arts – launched what would become a regular assembly of art makers and enjoyers in and around Digbeth. Local galleries get involved hosting exhibition openings and special performances in a variety of familiar and unlikely locations.

Address 19 Minerva Works, Fazeley Street, Birmingham B5 5RS, www.grand-union.org.uk |
Getting there Bus 97 to Fazeley Street, then a five-minute walk | Hours Wed–Sat
noon–5pm | Tip On nearby Banbury Street is the heavily fortified Proof House, an active
testing venue for gun barrels and ammunition. The Proof House has its own museum and
tour of the grounds; this requires booking 10 days in advance, and costs £200 for a party of
up to 10 people (www.gunproof.com).

50 Grazebrook Engine

Muscular powerhouse from the Steam Age

There's something about this landmark roundabout feature that hints at Birmingham's approach to heritage. This isn't a replica of a steam engine from the days of the Industrial Revolution, but the real thing. The twin-beam Grazebrook engine has Dudley origins, where it powered the bellows of two huge blast furnaces. Built according to James Watt's specification, it worked continuously for around a century.

Sentinel roundabout landmarks are something of a local tradition in the Midlands – variously you may encounter formations of Spitfires, a Chinese pagoda, or a giant Pegasus. Without intending to be so, the mighty Grazebrook engine has become art for cars. In a landscape of broadly similar dual carriageways and baffling roundabout exchanges, a glimpse of a familiar feature can help navigate more effectively than GPS. But shouldn't such a significant machine be in a museum rather than in the harsh roadside environment? What's more, this example turns out to be the largest steam engine ever made in Birmingham – a city founded on steam.

Few pedestrians treat the engine as a destination. A splash of daffodils and stepping stones across the grass acknowledge that some bolder tourists may be curious enough to arrive on foot. However, you won't be rewarded with any information other than the date (1817), which is cast into an iron panel on the engine's upper reaches. On close inspection, you'll see how this tough chunk of industrial hardware has weathered the elements over the years, with some original wooden and leather details still in place. It has been given a frame in blue engineering brick, which underlines its transformation from machine to art installation. This engine was built to last, and that is likely to be the take-away experience of your visit, whether you felt this was about industry, heritage, art or navigation.

Address Dartmouth Circus, Birmingham B6 4BE | **Getting there** Bus 65 or 67 to Dartmouth Circus | **Tip** The epic Wing Yip Superstore offers a huge selection of Oriental goods at 375 Nechells Park Road, Nechells. The owners gifted a pagoda to the city in 1998 (see ch. 26).

51 Great Stone Inn

How many stones in a pound?

Scattered across Birmingham's Rea Valley are a number of large boulders, which settled in the area having arrived from Wales around 400,000 years ago. The journey was slow, the stones having hitched a lift on the back of a glacier over the course of the last Ice Age. As the ice melted, the boulders were left across South Birmingham, later posing an enduring mystery to the geologists, who knew the stones were not indigenous. By necessity, the heavy stones were adapted into the local landscape (some feature in the tips within this book), and nowhere is this more visible than at the Great Stone Inn at Northfield.

The setting is unusually pastoral for Northfield's otherwise urban landscape, with a cluster of buildings here evoking a sense of a rural English village. The pub itself has a 15th-century timber frame, which was later built over completely in brick. The attractive, sandstone church of St Lawrence's opposite has a tower dating back to the 12th century. Round the corner from the pub is a former nailmaker's cottage with a pigeoncote incorporated into the chimney breast. The nail-making shed is still intact adjacent to the cottage. On the gable, the year 1750 is arranged in brick; easy to miss, but a helpful clue.

So where is the stone itself? For a long time, it lay on the ground at the corner of the pub facing the church, where it functioned as a butt stone. This was used by the old coaches, which put a back wheel against it to turn the tight corner, and further served to protect the building from accidental knocks. The enduring stone can now be found on the further side of the pub in what in the 17th century was the local pound for stray animals. The tough grey stone is a contrast to the soft pink sandstone of the pound. The stone now has an explanatory plaque: a consequence of local resident Roland Kedge's enthusiasm for geoheritage.

THE VILLAGE POUND
PROBABLY 17TH CENTURY

The Great Stone

This glacial erratic boulder was formed in an explosive volcanic eruption during the Ordovician period, 450-460 million years ago. During the ice age possibly up to 400,000 years ago, it was carried by an ice sheet from the Snowdon area of North Wales and deposited with many others around Northfield when the area was a frozen wasteland. For generations it lay at the corner of Church Road and Church Hill where it protected the Inn wall. The boulder was moved by Birmingham City Council to this site in 1954 for road safety reasons.

Address 158 Church Road, Northfield, Birmingham B31 2LU, +44(0)121 478 1254 | Getting there Bus 63 to Bell Lane, then an eight-minute walk | Hours Mon–Wed 11.30am–10.30pm, Thu–Sat 11.30am–11.30pm, Sun noon–10.30pm | Tip Visit the Great Stone Inn's beer garden, where another glacial erratic can be found resting on the lawn near to the pub (www.greatukpubs.co.uk).

52 Handsworth Old Town Hall

The Town Hall that was never a Town Hall

If you arrive on Slack Lane looking for a Town Hall, you will likely miss the two small timber-and-brick cottages that go by that name. The houses are supported by a cruck frame: an arch shape roughly hewn from an oak tree, with a limb projecting at roof height.

The curious name came sometime after 1460, when Handsworth was divided into eight 'ends', this building being in 'Town End'. A hall at that time could be any domestic residence, and was a step up from a lowly worker's humble home. Several alterations took place over the centuries, with the original wattle and daub panels being replaced with brick infills around 1625, and a chimney added around that time. What was originally a row of three houses was divided into two in the 20th century. The hall experienced an extended period of neglect, and narrowly avoided demolition. It can be enjoyed as an unexpected mediaeval encounter, a plot of rural Birmingham in a sprawling urban setting, or on one of the monthly open days you can visit the delightful community museum within.

The charming museum takes a grassroots approach, being the collections of various members of Handsworth Historical Society through the years. Downstairs are exhibition cases variously celebrating one member's love of Cadbury's chocolate, brands of yesteryear, and remembering the Festival of Britain. A map on the wall charts the location of the various farmhouses in the area, when the chief industry was agriculture. Upstairs, past the thick cruck joint, is a collection of 18th- and 19th-century silverware produced in Birmingham, an intricately rendered Victorian tithe map, antique typewriters and adding machines, a magic lantern, and Handsworth newspapers of the early 20th century. One collection is formed of the intriguing and sometimes mysterious contents of one member's aunt's kitchen cupboard.

Address 20 Slack Lane, Handsworth, Birmingham B20 2JN, +44 (0)121 747 5266, www.handsworth-historical-society.co.uk/home/old-town-hall | **Getting there** Bus 101 to College Road | **Hours** Open during monthly coffee mornings and by advance appointment – see website for details | **Tip** Mr Singh's Vegetarian Pizza at 103 Cornwall Road offers highly-regarded meat-free pizzas with an Indian spin (www.mrsinghspizza.co.uk).

53   Harborne Walkway

Railway line that became a park

Join Harborne Walkway at Summerfield Park near Edgbaston Reservoir, for a green and pleasant walk along a well-surfaced linear park of one-and-a-half miles. The route follows the trackbed of the railway line that originally ran from Birmingham New Street to Harborne, calling at seven stops along the way. The last passenger train ran in 1934, though the line still operated as a freight route until 1963. Visit Harborne library to see the original Harborne station platform sign.

The valley profile seen along sections of the walk suggests a tranquil, rural setting, but these are the overgrown embankments of the original line. Wooden railway sleepers among the vegetation show further evidence of the walkway's origins, as well as the regular brick viaducts. Some of these are ideal roosts for bats, and are kept dark for short sections for this reason, such as in the tunnel passing beneath Hagley Road. The walkway has its own code adopted by those choosing to be away from roads for the afternoon, or merely taking a shortcut, and you can expect a 'hello' from fellow walkers. Runners and cyclists know to 'share with care', but please be alert for bicycle bells. It is also a popular route for dog walkers.

You can take an optional detour to the recessed glade of Chad Brook walkway, where the route passes Woodbourne Road, before continuing through Harborne Nature Reserve and past the extensive allotments. Here, too, you can follow a path to a lower level and walk alongside Chad Brook (this is the route's soggiest section, so please choose appropriate footwear). As the route nears its end, the walkway is high above the surrounding landscape, giving an impressive bird's eye view of the woodland. Stop at the final elevated bridge for a chimney-top view of Harborne. From below, the heavily-braced bridge shows the effects of years of supporting the heavy iron steam trains.

Address Join Harborne Walkway near Selwyn Road, Birmingham B16 0SL, or from Forest Drive, Harborne B17 9HH | Getting there Bus 2 or 87 to Summerfield Park, then a five-minute walk | Tip A highlight on a street rich with refreshment options is the family-run Secret Sicilian restaurant at 73 High Street, Harborne. Hot drinks, wines and all-day Mediterranean dining with a Mediterranean courtyard (www.secretsicilian.com).

54 __ Hay Hall

Elizabethan hall marooned in industrial estate

Birmingham is known for its relentless, large-scale rebuilding projects, and as a result it's easy to forget that this was once a mediaeval town. However, dotted around the outer districts and suburbs are many well-preserved mediaeval and Tudor buildings, with some being open to the public. Notable among these are Blakesley Hall and Selly Manor, while some are less well known; indeed, Birmingham's oldest secular building is the Lad in the Lane pub in Erdington, which dates from 1400. Hay Hall, located in Hay Mills, is perhaps the most intriguing of these survivors.

An Elizabethan hall owned by the Este family, Hay Hall of today is conspicuously swallowed up by industry. The curious building now provides offices for the Reynolds Tube Company, makers of light-weight cycle frames. From the railings that fence off the Hay Hall industrial estate, you can see the slightly wonky form of a wealthy family home. It has undergone several alterations since being built in the 15th century, all adding to the intriguing story of this marooned renegade. The original timber structure was faced in brick in the 16th century, responding to fashionable materials of the day, and back then was the best way to flaunt your wealth. Hay Hall may even be Birmingham's oldest brick building. If you look closely, the lozenge patterns in the darker bricks are not regular, as if the bricklayers were still unfamiliar with the new technique.

The stone window jambs and mullions appear in different sizes and at different heights, and are likely made from the local sandstone. The wide chimney breast is a clue to the evolution of the chimney from being a separate chamber outside the building to a more discreet, integrated feature, seen here in a transitional stage. What now serves as a porch to the building was originally a projection built for a first floor latrine, with a chute to ground level.

Address Hay Hall Business Park, Redfern Road, Tyseley, Birmingham B11 2BE | Getting there Train to Tyseley, then an eight-minute walk | Tip Time your visit to coincide with an open day of active steam trains at Tyseley Locomotive Works (670 Warwick Road, www.vintagetrains.co.uk).

55 H B Sale

Birmingham's flatiron building

H B Sale is a curious wedge-shaped building with a tower, rising from a very narrow footprint. The unusual shape is a clue to the former high value of the land: any available plot capitalised on being in the right part of town. It is characterised by endless opulent detail, Gothic with Moorish and Oriental touches in rich red terracotta.

H B Sale is currently a Syrian restaurant, with nothing to indicate that it was formerly a diesinkers, specialising in stamping coins and tokens from metal. Architects William Doubleday and James R Shaw set out to demonstrate Birmingham's status as a wealthy international player, with every square foot embellished. Indeed, one latter-day name for this building was the Red Palace. No longer should factories be considered smoke-belching, functional mills – although this was usually what they were.

A plain fifth level was added in the 1960s, which shows how quickly notions of industrial pride changed in the 20th century. Surrounding buildings echo H B Sale's curved bullnose, and a 1990s apartment block includes a tribute tower faced in blue tile. The H B Sale tower is itself a tribute to the empire-extending military commander Lord Roberts, which is a clue to the colonial origins of Birmingham's wealth in 1895.

Moulded and fired terracotta became a surrogate for local sandstone, which, although a lovely salmon shade, tends to crumble. The solution was an industrial one: make an artificial version that's better than the original. Terracotta is seen all across Birmingham, most notably at the Victorian Law Courts, and its styling is specific enough to the city to have become known as Birmingham Gothic. Over a century later, much of this stonework is still in good condition, where it hasn't been deliberately chiselled off or destroyed by growth of wild-seeded trees. Another fine example is Martin and Chamberlain's Telephone Exchange (see ch. 12).

Address 1 Constitution Hill, Birmingham B19 3LG | Getting there Short walk from the city centre; bus 16 Platinum to Constitution Hill | Tip Walk further up Constitution Hill and Great Hampton Street to see more examples of Birmingham's proud manufactories: ornate brickwork, stained glass, and a cement pelican perched above an electroplater's workshop.

56 Highgate Windmill

Walsall's old-world industrial remnant

Despite its industrial heritage, Birmingham has no surviving windmills within its city boundaries. Or perhaps it is precisely because of its industrial success, with obsolete forms of power production quickly being replaced by the steam engine and its successors. It is to Walsall that the keen industrial researcher must head to find a surviving example.

The Old Windmill at Highgate looks as though it occupies a much earlier time, looming over a plot of land in Walsall's elevated Church Hill district. From some angles the windmill is invisible, and is easy to pass by, while from others it towers over the surrounding houses. Its sails have long gone and only a curious conical, brick tower remains. Later windows and crenelations only add to the mystery. Nearly lost under ivy is the original miller's cottage, standing where the garden joins the street. The wild setting and presence of antiquated iron gates and railings lend the encounter a sense of folklore or fairy tale.

The windmill dates back to the early 19th century, and after a short period of corn milling fell into disrepair. Its later adaptations capitalised on its lofty position in the town. In the later 19th century it was remodelled as a camera obscura, complete with fireplace and carpets, allowing views from four directions to be visible in one mirror. By 1925, it was remodelled as an observatory with a refracting telescope and a rotating platform that allowed the telescope to track stars through the night sky.

During the Second World War, the windmill's position suited its final transformation to a watch tower manned by Highgate's Air Raid Wardens. The tower stands on private grounds but a good view can be gained from the narrow alley that runs to the left of Fairfield Mount and connects Highgate Road with Folly House Lane, an address that surely references the later days of the tower.

Address 73 Highgate Road, Walsall WS1 3JB | **Getting there** Train to Walsall, then a 20-minute walk; bus 51 or X51 Platinum to Six Ways Walsall, then an 11-minute walk | **Tip** The New Art Gallery Walsall is home to the Garman Ryan Collection – a comprehensive collection of works by Jacob Epstein – as well as other modern and contemporary artists (Gallery Square, Walsall, www.newartgallerywalsall.org.uk).

57 Hockley Flyover Murals
What a relief!

Bold and mysterious shapes and forms line the vertical surfaces of Hockley Circus underpass. An organic accretion of symbols, cog teeth, stickles, nodes, nuts and bolts, egg boxes and coral reefs appear to grow from the walls around three subways. The abstract geometries hide some identifiable elements: a giant sunflower, the sawtooth outline of a large factory and the grottos, overhangs and headwalls of a craggy mountainscape.

The murals are the work of William Mitchell, an architectural sculptor with an international reputation for artistic expression in concrete. He poured this medium into highly modelled polyurethane moulds, often with pebble aggregate and pigments. He would then weather the cast surface with sandblasting and hammer blows. This technique quickly became the optimistic look of post-war Britain, appearing regularly in shopping centres and civic spaces. In 1968, people felt differently about the city's dramatic new environments, and the subways of Birmingham were ambitiously presented as places for creative engagement.

He may not have originally intended his works to be 'climbing walls for kids,' but after seeing his children's hands-on response, that's what they became. Children would routinely find their own adventures and escapades in urban spaces.

In later years, Mitchell created the Egyptian Hall and staircase at Harrods department store in London. Many see Aztec designs and ancient archetypes in his concrete murals, although Mitchell denied any conscious use of them in his patterns.

Sadly, the style's ubiquity meant it came to emphatically represent the past, not the future. Many examples were covered over, lost or destroyed, but with time, it has been possible to appreciate the style in the wider story of the 20th century. The murals achieved listed status in 2022… a great relief for the city's Modernism enthusiasts.

Address Access from Heaton Street, Birmingham B18 5BB | **Getting there** Buses 16 Platinum and 74 to Hockley Circus | **Tip** The Carnegie Infant Welfare Institute at 85 Hunters Road features an unusual painted mahogany sculpture of a mother and infant, titled *Maternity* and chiselled by William Bloye around 1926.

58 The Holdout Building

Sometimes less is more

A three-story brick building stands at 83 Newhall Street, currently occupied by Newhall Solicitors, and built in 1915 as a townhouse and surgery for the physician Samuel L Graham. It is discreet and dignified, its diamond brickwork offering a modest design flourish. Over the years, the building has been offices for a life assurance company, chartered surveyors and in more recent years a sequence of solicitors. Conspicuously, it is sandwiched between Canterbury House and Lancaster House, two large, multi-storey office blocks built in the 1950s and 1930s respectively.

The townhouse in its relationship to its neighbours is known as a 'holdout' building. The roofline of a city street can sometimes be read as a bar chart of economic growth: over time, buildings tend to get higher, then wider. For centuries, buildings were rarely more than two or three storeys, occupying long, narrow plots of land, with the short end meeting the street and therefore passers-by. As buildings gained height, developers bought up adjacent 'burgage' plots and demolished everything on them. Many parts of Birmingham's old town were lost in this way. Holdouts refuse to sell up to developers, and defiantly continue with business as usual, despite their uncomfortable-looking position. Occasionally one building will wholly engulf a holdout or leave it standing visibly marooned. The discrepancy in scale of the Newhall Street holdout serves as a powerful visual symbol for resilience and a challenge to the economic standard that bigger is better.

The arrangement prompts thoughts of human-scale architecture, harmonious townscape and of how buildings can provide trenchant metaphors for human characteristics. If you visit the Anchor Exchange shaft (see ch. 1) you can get a glimpse of the townhouse's garden space behind the vent, now occupied by an out-of-place building resembling a detached house.

Address 83 Newhall Street, Birmingham B3 1LH | Getting there Train to Snow Hill, then a five-minute walk; bus 22 or 23 to Colmore Row, then a five-minute walk | Tip Electrical retailer T C Hayes at 473 Bearwood Road has expanded from a small shop adjacent to Bearwood Causeway to now occupying all but one unit in that block. Their shop now forms a U-shape around D R Dalvair Pharmacy, the owners of which refuse an offer to sell up every few years.

59 — Industry and Genius

Tribute to an influential typographer

John Baskerville was perhaps the 18th century's most diverse industrialist: a gravestone carver, publisher, printer, keen-eyed typographer and successful businessman. His legacy is enduring, with the digital equivalent of his eponymous typeface still in use today on most word processing and design software platforms. Yet his presence in Birmingham is rarely seen directly. His catacombs grave is unmarked, while his portrait in the Museum and Art Gallery and his books in the Library of Birmingham can be viewed only by request. Standing in front of Baskerville House, David Patten's 1992 sculpture *Industry and Genius* is a rare instance of Baskerville's work being visibly celebrated.

The six Portland stone forms represent the letter punches used in the casting of printing type. The name Virgil, spelled out in reverse with bronze letters, references the Roman poet whose works Baskerville reprinted in 1750. His typeface acknowledges the Roman 'thick and thin' lettering style, and drew admiration from European influencers, putting Birmingham on the design map. The sculpture's site is significant, once being the grounds of Easy Hill, Baskerville's lavish country retreat. He lived his life against the grain, dressing flamboyantly and riding in a carriage drawn by white horses. He was open in his contempt for religion. When he died in 1775, his body was buried in his garden under a disused windmill to avoid a burial in hallowed ground.

Soon, industry swallowed up the once-rural house, and a canal was cut through the site of his mortal remains. These were shunted from vault to vault, unwelcome by the church that bore his ire, before finding some peace in the catacombs (see ch. 25). Perhaps Sir Arthur Conan Doyle borrowed Baskerville's name for his famous hell-hound? Maybe so, as that story features a clue gleaned by Sherlock Holmes' keen knowledge of contemporary newspaper fonts.

Address Baskerville House, Centenary Square, Birmingham B1 2ND | Getting there
Bus 23 to Baskerville House | Tip Sadly, Baskerville's wife Sarah was buried separately
in St Philips Cathedral grounds. Her grave can be found near the entrance at the top of
Cherry Street, behind the Workers' Memorial.

60 John Hall-Edwards Plaque

Remembering an X-Ray pioneer

Many of the blue plaques that appear on Birmingham's buildings incorporate the caveat 'on this site' or 'near here once stood' – a testament to the city's urgent need to rebuild itself. However, the plaque that memorialises John Hall-Edwards on the commanding Children's Hospital on Steelhouse Lane is the same building where Hall-Edwards worked as a radiologist – then called Birmingham General Hospital.

Hall-Edwards was an amateur photographer, and he brought this interest to his professional work as a physician. Initially this involved using microscopes, but in 1896 he used the X-ray technique – then called 'Roentgen rays' after discoverer Wilhelm Roentgen – to view a needle accidentally buried beneath a colleague's skin. This was just a few days after Roentgen had published his findings. A few weeks later, Hall-Edwards used X-rays to perform a surgical operation, which became the first medical use of X-rays anywhere. By 1899 he was the head radiologist at Birmingham General, and also at the city's Children's, Orthopaedic and Eye hospitals. His experiments were adopted quickly at other hospitals around the world, but his successes with the new technique came at a cost. With little known of the effects of X-rays in the early days, researchers and indeed patients became test subjects in what proved to be a harmful treatment if not properly screened. Hall-Edward lost his left arm and most of his right hand to the effects of X-rays, eventually succumbing to cancer in 1926.

During his life, Hall-Edwards was a respected figure in the city, actively working to promote scientific knowledge. He fiercely challenged the claims being made by his contemporary and fellow physician Sir Arthur Conan Doyle regarding the authenticity of photographs of the Cottingley Fairies, which appeared between 1917 and 1920, at a time when many were keen to believe.

Address Steelhouse Lane, Birmingham B4 6NH | **Getting there** Tram to Bull Street | Tip Another of Hall-Edwards' Victorian hospitals is still standing, and like Birmingham Children's Hospital, is architecturally rich. Head to the Hotel du Vin on Church Street to see what was once the Birmingham and Midland Eye Hospital.

61 Kardomah Café
Home of Birmingham Surrealism

Kardomah Cafés comprised a luxurious chain of coffee outlets across England and Wales (and one in Paris), seeing their heyday in the first half of the 20th century. They were popular haunts for the artists and writers of the city, who, for an affordable price, were able to meet or work in inspiring environments. In Birmingham, the local Kardomah was the favourite destination for the local Surrealist group, regularly meeting here in the 1940s and 50s. The Kardomah closed in 1970, but echoes of its illustrious past are still evident.

The Birmingham Surrealists had amongst their number Conroy Maddox, a writer and collagist inspired by Max Ernst, the poet and artist Emmy Bridgwater, and brothers John and Robert Melville, a painter and an art critic respectively. In 1948 they were joined by Desmond Morris, just out of his teens and already dedicated to the Surrealist cause. As a student at the University of Birmingham, he once found a discarded elephant's skull behind the zoology department. He then left it in a shop doorway on Broad Street, to the bafflement of the public and the local newspaper, who thought they had found a dinosaur. Morris went on to become a celebrated zoologist and writer, and in 2023 is still producing his surreal landscapes, populated by the organic forms he calls biomorphs and reminiscent of Yves Tanguy.

Tantalisingly, the plump terracotta scrolls lining the outside of the café's arched windows, and the writhing serpentine forms in the first-storey cornice, look like they could be straight from Morris's surreal landscapes. The faded Kardomah Café sign can still be discerned in the cartouche above the door to 42a New Street, while inside, the fireplace, wooden stairs and decorative plaster panels date to the time of the Kardomah. The café's colourful, floral mosaic occupies the entire length of the upper floor of Charles Tyrwhitt at 41 New Street.

Address 41 and 42a New Street, Birmingham B2 4EG | Getting there Train to New Street; tram to Grand Central; various buses to the city centre | Hours ECCO at 42a New Street is currently open Mon–Sat 9.30am–5.30pm, Sun 11am–5pm; Charles Tyrwhitt at 41 New Street is open Mon–Sat 10am–6pm, Sun 11am–5pm | Tip The Birmingham Surrealists appreciated a good mosaic and would also meet round the corner at The Trocadero pub on Temple Street, which features a colourful glazed facade, and a sign formed of red, yellow and green mosaic tiles.

62 The Kennedy Memorial
Celebrating an Irish Quarter idol

The large, colourful mosaic on the corner of Floodgate Street and High Street, Deritend, depicts the 35th President of the USA, John F Kennedy, meeting a large, enthusiastic crowd in front of the White House. Hands and hats are raised in support of the popular president, eyes and smiles wide. Supporters include Martin Luther King Jr, and the president's brother, Teddy.

JFK was America's first Irish-Catholic president, and Birmingham's Irish community regarded him as a paragon of pride and success. The loss was keenly felt on his assassination, and in 1968 a mosaic was commissioned to memorialise him, paid for by public prescription. This memorial is neither the original mosaic, nor the original location, however. The first mosaic, by Kenneth Budd, was installed in the pedestrian subway island near St Chad's Roman Catholic Cathedral, where it remained until 2007. The subway was eventually filled in, and rumours circulated that the mosaic had been saved and stored, awaiting a suitable new home. However, what you see on Floodgate Street is an entirely new recreation by Kenneth Budd's son, Oliver.

If you imagine you have joined the crowd, positioned somewhere behind the burly policeman, and spend time surveying the landscape, another story emerges. Playing in the background to the left of the president are his wife and children; to the right are sinister, green policemen confronting a crowd with snarling dogs and raised truncheons. Everyone in the crowd to the right of a certain vertical axis looks troubled or distracted, one man is even smiling and frowning at once. The pattern on Teddy Kennedy's forehead as he looks into the distance seems to take on a target shape, as if having a premonition of his brother's assassination. Also in this darker section is former Lord Mayor Mike Nangle, who requested his own likeness be included somewhere in the new mosaic.

Address Corner of Floodgate Street and High Street, Deritend, Birmingham B5 5SU |
Getting there Bus 3, 4 or 5 to South & City College | Tip The Spotted Dog, on the corner
of Alcester Street, is Digbeth's best Irish pub, with regular live music, a roaring fire, and
large covered outdoor area.

63 Kilder
Underneath the arches

Just down the passage from the Alfa Romeo garage, and once their scrap and spares store, lies Kilder, embedded neatly into an arch in the viaduct that brings trains into Moor Street Station. This craft beer bar operates in tandem with Original Patty Men, the burger bar in the next unit. Originally, Kilder was a place to get a beer while waiting for space in OPM to become available, but is now a destination in its own right. It's an artful use of space that feels snug and secure, so long as you don't mind the occasional clang and churn of the steel wheels arriving above.

The name Kilder derives from Kilderkin, a huge, 18-gallon beer cask; and beer is Kilder's main game. Around a dozen draught beers are always on tap and in constant rotation, with Siren's Santo being the only constant. Sours are a regular favourite. While the ale's strength can climb to sippable-only levels, there are always 2–3% table beers on hand. Kilder features regular tap takeovers from craft ale brewers from around the UK and beyond. Kilder is further a rarity in that it serves a selection of cocktails on draught, a uniquely industrial solution.

Despite its deeply vaulted location, the cavernous room is surprisingly light. One single expanse of metal-framed door and window occupies the open end of the arch. Kilder's interior was styled by Birmingham designers Faber, who acknowledged the industrial setting, while also managing to give it a sleek and light utilitarian look. The arch theme appears around the bar, including the in-house typography. The owners of Kilder are film fans at heart, and have introduced the concept of pairing food with films at a time when pairing food with beer is still gaining traction. A screen descends to block out the light from the window, and the vault becomes a cinema auditorium. *Goodfellas* with spaghetti and sauce? It's the city's Italian influence again.

Address 5 Shaw's Passage, Birmingham B5 5JG, +44 (0)121 643 2546, www.kilderbar.co.uk |
Getting there Train to Moor Street, or to New Street, then an eight-minute walk;
various buses to Moor Street | Hours Wed & Thu 5–11pm, Fri & Sat noon–11pm, Sun
noon–10pm | Tip Digbeth Community Gardens, opposite, is an open and active urban
green space championing plants for food and nature, and hosting regular art events (see
www.digbethcommunitygarden.wordpress.com for events and opening times).

64 Kingsbury Water Park

A day out to Birmingham's Lake District

Kingsbury Water Park is an extensive water feature shaped not by river or glacial erosion, but by industry – in more than one sense. The water park is a series of pools and lakes of varying sizes scattered across the landscape just east of the M6 Toll road, like a floodplain between the river Tame and the Birmingham and Fazeley Canal. The curious shape of some of the pools hints that this is not a natural feature but rather a series of depleted gravel pits, flooded for leisure use.

Unlike the UK's port cities, or those built on mighty rivers, Birmingham thrived due to its proximity to the coal mines that fuelled the industry upon which it grew. An ambitious canal network stood in for its modest rivers, leading to a thriving economy and city expansion, but also an absence of water features. Birmingham is as far as it's possible to get from the coast in the UK, so when towpaths and reservoirs are insufficient to quench residents' aquatic requirements, Kingsbury is their destination. It's ideal for bird spotters, too, with three hides around the pools, and a wide variety of water birds nesting or visiting. Anglers are also welcome, and visitors can even hire a variety of vehicles, ranging from bikes to boats to jet skis. Follow the river Tame further north to Cliff Lakes for water-skiing lessons. Perhaps the best way to explore the lakes, however, is by foot along the many paths that meander between the pools. The low horizon and irregular pools mean it's easy to become disorientated, but for many that's part of the attraction.

The nearly village of Kingsbury has some intriguing mediaeval survivors, with the tranquil 12th-century church of St Peter and St Paul, and a fortified manor house with its imposing sandstone curtain wall still intact. The wider landscape is threaded with brooks and ponds, and invites exploration – just be sure to bring your Ordnance Survey map.

Address Bodymoor Heath, Sutton Coldfield B76 0DY, www.countryparks.warwickshire.gov.uk | Getting there 20 minutes by car via the M6; an hour by bicycle along the Birmingham and Fazeley canal towpath from Newhall Street | Tip Middleton Hall and Gardens is a complex of mediaeval, Tudor and Georgian buildings and a walled garden, with shops and a café. It can be found at Middleton, Tamworth.

65 Lapworth Geology Museum

Let's rock

A huge allosaurus greets you at the door, swinging its bony tail high, ready to jab the eye of the skeletal pteranodon in hot pursuit. This is the Lapworth Museum of Geology, perfect for those wanting to better understand the features and processes of the earth, and honouring the legacy of the geologist Charles Lapworth.

In the late 19th century, Lapworth pioneered research into Silurian beds, and his ability to locate water beneath the Birmingham bedrock meant he was regularly in demand by industrialists. Prehistoric evidence at the museum is sourced from around the world, but it also has a local outlook, from a time when Birmingham had a climate comparable with that of the Bahamas. Here are the fossilised trail of footprints left by Ichniotherium in Shropshire, and the insect-like trilobites known locally as Dudley Bugs (see ch. 111). There are hints of the museum's own history in the many cabinets of curiosities, heavy wooden remnants that have been adapted to include dinoscapes in their lower sections for curious kids.

The rock wall feature comprises 125 specimens in a towering display cabinet on a specially strengthened floor, which allows the rocks to be enjoyed in their essence with minimal labelling. Upstairs is the astonishing mineral case, luxuriating in the colours, textures and forms before highlighting the specimens' scientific properties. This floor explores the scientific properties of gemstones and minerals and in a darkened corner of the room, examples of fluorescence in minerals.

Keep an eye out for Lapworth Lates: evening events featuring diverse speakers, artists, ceramicists and dancers responding to the collection, as well as cutting-edge research from the University of Birmingham's dinosaur research group.

Address Aston Webb A Block Building, Ring Road South, University of Birmingham, Edgbaston, Birmingham B15 2TT, www.birmingham.ac.uk/facilities/lapworth-museum/index.aspx | **Getting there** Train from New Street to University; bus 61 or 62 to Bristol Road, then a five-minute walk | **Hours** Mon–Fri 10am–6pm, Sat & Sun noon–5pm | **Tip** Behind the nearby Bramhall Music Building and just across Ring Road South lies a glacial erratic, namely a rock relocated here by a glacier during the last ice age.

66 Last Public Hanging
Grisly memorial in a grim setting

The site of Birmingham's last public hanging is in a suitably grim location: a dingy ring road tunnel beneath a viaduct, conspicuously outside the keenly maintained Colmore Business District. The silver plaque is duct taped to the crumbling white, glazed bricks in the upper reaches of the tunnel wall. If anyone hurrying through spots it as it catches a shaft of daylight from above, they will learn that this was the site of the final moments of local gangster, Philip 'Drake' Matsell.

Matsell came from Yarmouth and ran away to sea aged 15. After arriving in Birmingham, he fell in with a disreputable gang. On the night of 18 July, 1806, he shot and wounded the peace officer Robert Twyford, who approached a group of men he thought may be breaking into a house. Initially, his sentence was deportation to Australia, but having been apprehended after attempting to escape, he was sentenced to death by hanging at the site of the murder. An 1880 account describes his mile-long procession from Camp Hill to Snow Hill, bound by his executioner to a black, open cart, which also carried his coffin. There he was met by a 'dense crowd of 50,000 people', who jeered, cursed and sobbed as he kicked his boots into the crowd, and with a bold cry of 'here goes', leapt into the air from the 20-foot gibbet, which was wheeled in for the occasion.

While the plaque refers to the murder of Twyford, later research has shown that he recovered from the wound. The plaque could equally have read Birmingham's 'first' or 'only' public hanging, as it was Gallows Hill in Stoneleigh, near Warwick Assizes, that locals were usually sent to be hanged. If the estimation of the large crowd is accurate, then more than half of the town showed up for the execution. This fact, and the dark theatre of the long public procession, suggest that this hanging was intended to discourage other bad characters of the town from villainy.

Address Tunnel beneath the Snow Hill line viaduct on Great Charles Street, Birmingham B3 | Getting there Train or tram to Snow Hill or walk from Livery Street | Tip A quarter of a mile away, an earlier plaque also makes a (false) claim for the notorious site. Now the Actress and Bishop, The Last Drop pub was named after the hanging, while slyly suggesting a drained drink.

67 Legend of St Kenelm

Celtic tradition lives on beyond the churchyard

St Kenelm's is a charming church located in the Clent hills, featuring a wealth of original Norman masonry, weathered grotesques and gargoyles, and showcasing the region's bright red sandstone. A footpath to the right takes you down through a leafy dell, past horsetails and nettles into a tranquil glade rich with tradition and legend. This charged spot is both the source of the river Stour and, according to legend, the site where Kenelm, Prince of Mercia, was murdered and buried around AD 820.

When King Kenwulf died in AD 819, he left two daughters and a young son. Sister Cwendrida wanted to reign as queen, and conspired with their guardian, Askbert, to kill her young brother, Kenelm. The first effort was thwarted, and Kenelm produced a great ash tree from a staff he stuck into the ground. On the second attempt, Askbert sliced off his head, then buried the body in a thicket. The story goes that news was conveyed to Rome by a dove carrying a note in its beak. Accordingly, the Pope wrote to English royalty about the wrongdoing, and the body was promptly uncovered and re-buried in Winchelcombe, Gloucestershire.

A carved wooden figure of the boy king with magic staff and the messenger bird appears above the lych gate on entering the churchyard. The holy spring follows a short stone culvert to a squat, mossy stone wall with a plaque acknowledging the significance of the site. Follow the wooden walkway round to the right and you will encounter a raggedy bush. For generations, a hawthorn tree here has been tied with rags, pendants, items of jewellery and charms, all having significance to those who place them. These curative trees sometimes appear near holy wells associated with saints, but perpetuate a much earlier pagan tradition. A rag would be dipped in the well then tied to the tree, in the belief that as the material weathered the ailment would fade.

Address St Kenelm's Church, Romsley, Halesowen B62 0NG | Getting there Bus 9 to Halesowen, then bus 4H to Mendip Road, then a 30-minute walk | Tip Even further out into the Staffordshire countryside are the Rock Houses of Kinver Edge: sandstone cave homes visitable at Holy Austin Rock House, Compton Road, Kinver, Stourbridge (www.nationaltrust.org.uk/kinver-edge-and-the-rock-houses).

68 The Lock-Up

Steelhouse Lane's historic mini prison

West Midlands Police Museum has steadily grown since it began in 1964 as a resource in the Tally Ho Police Training Centre in Edgbaston. This collection of memorabilia merged with artefacts from the Forensic Science Service laboratory, before opening as a public museum in Sparkhill Police Station in 1993. When Steelhouse Lane Police Station closed to the public in 2017, the museum started running open days and events out of the station's now empty Central Custody Suite, and building work separated it from the police station.

This Victorian 'mini-prison' had space for 70 detainees over three storeys, connected by iron staircases and clanking walkways. The whitewashed, windowless walls, stark cells and unforgiving wooden cell doors are largely unchanged since 1891. The basement level has a white-tiled tunnel that leads directly and securely to the Victoria Law Courts, so those charged with an offence could head directly to court from their cell. The West Midlands Police Museum features exhibitions drawing from the police archives, including old newspaper reports, vintage police equipment and criminal mugshots, which naturally includes Peaky Blinders and other Birmingham gangsters. Recent additions to the collection are the various knuckle dusters, knives and cigarettes found hidden behind the cells' heating grills down the years, revealed during recent building work.

As well as the artefacts collection, the museum reveals the development of forensic evidence from a pre-fingerprint age to advances in DNA profiling. The museum hosts regular open days, talks and hands-on activities, and is actively researching its own collection. A key aspect of the museum's approach is to address how policing has changed over the years, reflecting changes in social attitudes and tackling notorious police controversies, such as the overturned convictions of the Birmingham Six.

Address Steelhouse Lane, Birmingham B4 6BJ, +44 (0)345 113 5000, www.wmpeelers.com | Getting there Train to Snow Hill | Hours Tue–Sun 10am–4pm | Tip Behind the lock-up and at the heart of the legal district are The Victoria Law Courts on Corporation Street, with endless detail to be found in the epic drama of the rich red terracotta.

69 Lucifer

'Better to reign in Hell than serve in Heaven'

An 11-foot statue of the fallen angel Lucifer greets visitors to the Birmingham's Museum and Art Gallery. He towers over visitors, bronze wings outstretched, delicately dipping his toe into the fiery lake, and with his male member conspicuously free of his barely-real skirts. The figure conveys many apparent contradictions. This curious vision of Lucifer is proudly and visibly androgynous. His or her wings appear rather solid for an angel, and are seemingly attached to the body by means of a chest band. A scar encircles the angel's midriff. The female face is that of regular life model Sunita, who creator Jacob Epstein had previously rendered as a Madonna.

The story of Lucifer's arrival in Birmingham after a high profile expulsion from Heaven can be traced back to 1944 and Epstein's desire to find a public home for his new sculpture. The buyer was A W Lawrence, brother of T E Lawrence ('of Arabia'), but a public gallery space was not immediately forthcoming. The Fitzwilliam in Cambridge, the V&A and Tate in London each had their own reasons for not accepting the gift, while simply not knowing what to make of Epstein's controversial new work. The Tate's rejection sparked publicity that led to Manchester and Liverpool galleries showing interest, but Birmingham – perhaps with an eye for valuable metal – got there first.

Apart from a spell in the sidelines of the Edwardian Tea Rooms, Lucifer has enjoyed a glorious reign in the Round Room ever since. Indeed, Birmingham has long welcomed citizens from diverse cultures, nationalities and religious beliefs. Nearby street names seem to foreshadow Lucifer's arrival: Eden Place is a narrow passage behind the museum, while near to the ring road is the vestigial fragment of Paradise Circus. This last hints at John Milton's epic poem Paradise Lost, which inspired Epstein in the lead up to his rebellious creation.

Address Museum & Art Gallery, Chamberlain Square, Birmingham B3 3DH, +44 (0)121 348 8000, www.birminghammuseums.org.uk | **Getting there** Train to New Street, then a 10-minute walk; buses to Colmore Row | **Hours** Daily 10am–5pm. Please note that the Museum and Art Gallery is closed for extensive maintenance until 2024. | **Tip** Dating from around AD 600 and discovered during the construction of the East India railway in 1861, the Sultanganj Buddha was shipped to Birmingham to provide inspiration for metalworkers. The statue can be found in room 20.

70_Mary Vale Road
ABC Houses
A gazetteer of Victorian destinations

Taking a stroll along Mary Vale Road from Stirchley to Bournville is to read a historical document of possible destinations from late-Victorian Birmingham. Most of the houses on the left-hand side were named after towns in the UK, a few after European cities, and even Odessa, then in Imperialist Russia. These may have been reached on foot, by bicycle or more likely by train: indeed, it was because the railways had opened up the country that any consideration of going to most of these places was possible. The nearest-named is Harborne, just three miles away, which would also be the destination for any residents who enjoyed a drink: founded by Quakers, Bournville was alcohol-free, and remains so today. Frankley and Tyseley (here misspelled 'Tysley') also appear.

Other house names are suggestions of days out by train to towns with a castle or abbey, such as Tutbury and Tintern, or are coastal resort towns, such as Cromer. Some sections are arranged alphabetically, reverse alphabetically, or thematically, such as a cluster of Irish locations, including Wicklow, Kenmare, Maynooth, Tyrone and (the river) Boyne. This may have been to welcome Irish workers to the area, or to acknowledge that many of those who built these dwellings were likely Irish. There's also a cluster of European cities beginning with V – Venice, Vienna, Valencia and Verona – which may appeal to the more adventurous, and perhaps wealthier, traveller.

Puzzlingly, some names don't seem to refer to real places, such as Altador and Urngrove, though the latter has a bas-relief of an urn in the decorative stone lintel. Look closely, and you will see lions, frowning faces and pagan images of the Green Man hidden amongst the carved foliage. It's interesting to see how some residents have embellished the stones with their own colour themes, or adapted them, such as the painted apple at Bramley.

Address Mary Vale Road, Bournville, Birmingham B30 2DN | Getting there Train to Bournville; bus 45 or 47 to Hazelwell Street | Tip Another set of alphabetical houses from Astley to Jarrow runs from 938–1036 Pershore Road.

71 Medicine Bakery & Gallery

Artisan bakery, café and gallery

Easy to miss among the well-known coffee shops and baguette outlets of New Street is the entrance to Medicine Bakery and Gallery. A handsome wooden door studded with brass rosettes leads up a wood-panelled stairway. At the top of the stairs, in a white-tiled and plant-enriched lobby, you'll be greeted by a selection of donuts, cakes and pastries, open sandwiches and loaves, all baked in-store.

Many visitors come just for the excellent bakery products, but beyond is the unexpected presence of the two-story exhibition space formerly used by the Royal Birmingham Society of Artists, which dates back to 1912. Medicine's interior design responds to the light, airy nature of the space. Antique mirrors reflect its history, while large, lush pot plants stand in the floor space, hang from ceilings and occupy the height of the far wall. Dried flowers and grasses complement the verdant theme. The variety of tables means you can dine in comfort on the upholstered seating around the edge, grab a single table to catch up with some work, or spread out in a group around the larger tables with benches. Many RBSA members come here to remember their favourite space. The gallery is top-lit by large windows set in the vaulted ceiling that maximise the wall space. Several artists are usually on display, and the exhibitions often rotate, with regular evening opening events.

Parallel with the gallery is the café, open for brunch and lunch, with brioche dishes from the bakery a speciality, and a fine line in Benedicts. Many find the generous space conducive to work, while enjoying coffee and a cake. The dual nature of the space means you may need to be considerate to anyone who happens to be dining under your favourite painting. When descending the stairway as you leave, look for the 'ghosts' of RBSA members in the traces of the letters of their names which once adorned the panels.

Address 69a New Street, Birmingham B2 4DU, +44 (0)121 643 1188, www.medicinebakery.co.uk | **Getting there** Trains to New Street; buses to the city centre | **Hours** Daily 8.30am–5pm | **Tip** The RBSA is still very active, having relocated to the Jewellery Quarter in 2000. The gallery showcases the arts and crafts of members, runs workshops and sells prints, ceramics and jewellery from the in-house shop (4 Brook Street, www.rbsa.org.uk).

72 Metchley Fort
What have the Romans ever done for Birmingham?

In 2015, during tram-line excavations in the city centre, a section of cobbled road was discovered at the top of Hill Street, which the local newspaper suggested was of Roman origin. Birmingham post-dates the Roman occupation by many centuries, but nevertheless an Ancient Roman presence can still be detected in parts of the city.

Around AD 48, a Roman garrison was stationed near what is now the Queen Elizabeth Hospital; its Roman name is unknown, but it has acquired the name Metchley. It was built to keep marauding early Britons out of the Roman-secured strongholds in the north. The significant location was at once a tribal boundary, close to a water source (the Bournbrook) and formed the crossroads of Roman roads from Droitwich, Alcester and Letocetum, now called Wall in Staffordshire. The undulating grassy landscape here is a reconstruction of the defensive troughs and ramparts of the original fort, resembling ancient barrows.

A 20th-century dig revealed Metchley to be a permanent fort for around 1,000 soldiers, with wooden outer defensive walls and an inner compound of buildings, including a stable, granary and barracks. Also made visible here in brick is the route of the epic Roman road Icknield Street, glimpsed briefly before heading straight through to Sutton Park, where it is clearly visible for a one-and-a-half-mile section (see ch. 104).

Roman coins and beads are occasionally discovered along the road, and at Metchley, pottery vessels from England and France were unearthed, along with brooches and a curious bronze cast of a dog. In 2000, the layout of a vicus was uncovered, this being a pop-up village populated by native Britons, providing cooked food for the soldiers. Tantalisingly, what appear to be ancient timbers amongst the hillocks nearest the hospital are in fact the remains of a reconstruction of one of the fort's towers, dating back only a few decades.

Address Visible and accessible from the Medical School, University of Birmingham, Edgbaston, Birmingham B15 2TT | Getting there Train from New Street to University | Tip Metchley Abbey was the picturesque Gothic former home of composer Sir Granville Bantock at 93 Metchley Lane.

73 Midland Bank Demon

Stone-faced satire of Victorian fat cats

In a society obsessed with smartphones, few of us have the presence of mind to glance upwards now and then. Those who do so in Birmingham could be rewarded by the strong-featured Grecian fellow with flowing locks, located in the keystone above the doorway to this former bank. His most distinctive feature is neither his aquiline nose nor his abundant beard, but a pair of helically intertwined horns sprouting from his head. The horns are decoratively plaited, almost like a headpiece, while he gazes into the distance, as if surveying the extent of his domain. On closer inspection, the horns are open-ended like cornucopias, but instead of spilling harvest bounty, out pour many coins decorated with crests, emblems and royal profiles, which merge with his ringlets and beard.

This figure may seem a curious way to greet customers to the Midland Bank. Who is he and what does his approach to money represent? The Victorians were fond of demonstrating their wealth through opulent design and architectural enrichment, and all UK cities feature buildings with classical references. However, this character doesn't feature in Greek or Roman mythology. Instead, his presence seems to be a subtle satire by the architect Edward Holmes on Victorian bankers' excessive wealth and their focus on riches – a satire that could equally hold true for the British Empire and, indeed, for any successive wealthy tenants of the building. It was not unheard of for Victorian architects to prank their clients in their way, and was also evident in Watson Fothergill's stone monkeys for the Nottingham and Nottinghamshire Bank: a 'stone monkey' was a term for a mortgage.

While we may admire Holmes' audacious spoof, as an architect for a banking company he was likely a wealthy man himself. Whether his clients disapproved, were amused by, or even noticed his efforts, we can only speculate.

Address 128 New Street, Birmingham B2 4DB | Getting there Short walk from the city centre | Tip Another elevated sculpture is William Bloye's bas-relief for the Sun Insurance office at 9–10 Bennetts Hill.

74__Moor Pool Estate
The secret garden suburb

Garden suburbs are carefully planned estates on the outskirts of a city, which balance generous housing, open space, leisure amenities and agriculture. These estates became popular in the social reforms of the late Victorian and Edwardian period. Birmingham's most visible garden suburb is Bournville – known as the factory in a garden – but the Moor Pool Estate is a lost delight just a few minutes' walk from Harborne High Street.

Moor Pool was the vision of Birmingham philanthropist John Sutton Nettlefold and his appointed architect, Frederick Martin. It represents early advances in town planning. 500 houses were built between 1907 and 1912, appearing just a few years after Bournville, and intended to give affordable, low-density homes to a mix of manual workers, artisans and prosperous professionals. Little has changed over the decades, and Moor Pool became a conservation zone in 1970. To stroll around Moor Pool today is to experience the same thoughtful charm it had when new. Houses are in the Arts and Crafts tradition, and while Moor Pool has a consistent architectural language, no two houses are exactly the same. Most homes have a two-tone appearance: red brick on the ground floor with a cream stucco first floor, placing it somewhere between the whitewashed walls of the Calthorpe Estate (see ch. 22) and the more usual material of Birmingham buildings.

Especially intriguing are the dwellings on Ravenhurst Road opposite the original duck pond of Moor Pool. These houses feature arrow-slit windows and entry by bridge from the pavement directly to the first floor, as if over a moat. Streets are tree-lined, with grass verges and green open spaces. At the centre is The Circle, with community shops and the original sports facilities: tennis courts, a snooker club, skittles, a bowling green, and – in contrast to the peaceful surroundings – an air rifle and pistol club.

Address Streets surrounding The Circle, Harborne B17 9DY | Getting there Buses 23 or 24 to Harborne High Street, then a 10-minute walk | Tip Away from Harborne's vibrant High Street is The Bell, a 300-year-old farmhouse-turned-pub in a curiously rural setting (11 Old Church Road, Harborne).

75 Moseley Dovecote
18th-century tower in a peaceful setting

Two bold brick buildings set in a well-appointed herb garden greet anyone strolling from Moseley to Kings Heath. The tall, octagonal tower is the dovecote, and nearby is the cowhouse. They are outbuildings of Moseley Hall, an 18th-century country house now buried within the hospital complex further down the hill. The compact 'cowhouse', despite its local nickname, was actually a hay barn featuring air holes to prevent the hay self-combusting.

For its small scale, it is actually a three-storey structure, with a wooden staircase leading to the first floor. Recessed Romanesque arches give the impression of windows, and diamond-shaped vents set into the brickwork break up the expanse of the walls. An octagonal aperture at the roof's apex admits the doves into their shadowy domain, and is topped by an ironwork finial. Why keep doves? Once thought to be an ingredient for pigeon pies to be served at the hall, it is now recognised that doves' meat is rather tough, and only the young squabs would be eaten. This was a prestigious luxury food, and visibly positioning a dovecote near the road would have been a gesture of status. If the eggs were ever eaten it would have been for medicinal reasons only.

The dovecote sits within a recreation of an 18th century garden, featuring the flowers, herbs, fruits and plants contemporary to the time. Beyond the garden, some of the Victorian houses on Alcester Road and deeper into Moseley feature octagonal towers at their corners, perhaps inspired by the dovecote. The garden is now used by patients and visitors to the hospital as a place for tranquillity and reflection, and can also be visited by passers-by. The best time to visit is on one of the regular open days, when an exhibition inside the tower illustrates the history and role of dovecotes. In the upper reaches of the tower, 'clay pigeons' stand in for the doves that once nested here.

Address 179 Alcester Road, Moseley, Birmingham B13 8JR, www.moseley-society.org.uk/news-events-2/dovecote | **Getting there** Bus 1, 35 or 50 to Moseley Village | **Hours** See website for current information on visiting | **Tip** The Ice House is a contemporary of Moseley Dovecote, and demonstrates how food was kept chilled in the 18th century. Open on selected Sundays in Moseley Park on Alcester Road.

76 Moseley Road Baths

Victorian pools swimming against the current

Moseley Road Baths is part of a cluster of civic buildings in Balsall Heath, dating from Victorian and Edwardian times. Back then, the corporation regularly paired swimming baths with libraries, and across the road there is also the former School of Art, forming a harmonious hub of hygiene, fitness, knowledge and creative expression. In recent years, the baths have regularly faced closure. Birmingham can be quite unsentimental about its past, and the corporation saw them as outdated, with more modern pools being provided elsewhere. Locals recognised that the baths were about much more than slick facilities, and their determination and sustained community spirit have kept the baths afloat.

Today, the baths function as an active swimming resource, a location for arts events, as well as an intriguing urbex option. Public baths in Edwardian times existed primarily for hygiene, dating from a time when few people had a bath in their home. Communal swimming for exercise and relaxation was just one available option: bathers may prefer an individual 'slipper bath', which is to say a single bath that would be partially covered over to keep in the heat, and resembling a slipper in appearance. Different levels of luxury were available to bathers wishing to pamper themselves.

Regular guided tours take visitors behind the scenes to visit the various historical bathing options, the evocative steam-punk of the gas-fired boiler rooms, the huge iron water tanks, and the abandoned caretaker's lodge and storage rooms in the upper reaches of the building, scattered with clues of their former use. The baths regularly host adventurous cultural events, such as synchronised swimming, screenings for a floating audience courtesy of Flatpack Film Festival, sound installations curated by digital artist Leon Trimble, and swimming to soundtracks provided by Birmingham's heavy metal champions and curators, Home of Metal.

Address 497 Moseley Road, Balsall Heath, Birmingham B12 9BX, +44 (0)121 439 0320, www.moseleyroadbaths.org.uk | Getting there Bus 50 to St Paul's Road | Hours See website for current events timetable | Tip Across the road at 496 Moseley Road is Ort Gallery, an artist-led exhibition space closely embedded in the community and making local culture visible (www.ortgallery.co.uk).

77__Mothers

Listen with Mothers

Every generation, Birmingham produces a rock club that challenges the capital city, and draws in crowds from miles around. Today, that magnet is the annual Supersonic Festival, and in the late 1970s and early 1980s it was the Rum Runner – famous for producing pop legend Duran Duran. In the late 1960s, however, that cultural force was Mothers in Erdington.

The club was located above a modest furniture store and a gentleman's outfitters, taking over from the long-established dance venue, The Carlton Ballroom. Mothers was an enduringly popular destination despite being some distance outside the city centre. A visit to the location today belies the importance and excitement of the time, but for over two years Mothers was considered the best music venue in the country. Its live programme read like a Who's Who of Rock, with artists playing there including acts such as Led Zeppelin, King Crimson, Jethro Tull, Elton John and Tyrannosaurus Rex. One side of Pink Floyd's 1969 album *Ummagumma* was recorded at Mothers earlier that year, and the band's drummer, Nick Mason, was born in Birmingham. Soft Machine's album *Third* has live music recorded at Mothers. The Who performed the entirety of their rock opera *Tommy*, and Birmingham band Traffic played their debut gig at the venue. Black Sabbath were regular attendees, as well as fellow founders of heavy metal, Judas Priest. The club would receive regular promotion by BBC radio DJ John Peel, a champion of provincial happenings, and a regular DJ at the club.

Today, the space once occupied by the venue is now a discount outlet for beds, curtains and rugs, with only the clearance beanbags to hint at its 60s heyday. Outside, Mothers is memorialised by a blue plaque, although careless whitewashing of the wall has rendered the text unreadable, as if to say 'If you remember the 60s, you weren't there'.

Address 185 High Street, Erdington, Birmingham B23 6SY | Getting there Train to
Erdington, then a 10-minute walk; bus X4 Platinum or X5 Platinum to Barnabas Road |
Tip Bleak Hill Park on Short Heath Road begins an unexpectedly green, mile-long walk
through to Witton Lakes.

78 Museum Collection Centre

An epic collection of collections

From the outside, the Museum Collection Centre looks much like any of its industrial warehouse neighbours, variously trading in welding, flooring and hot sauce solutions. The rubbish skips of Dollman street belie the wealth of treasures available within the vast storeroom. All municipal museums have them: storage areas large enough to accommodate the combined material that doesn't make it into the public galleries and display cases, which can be as much as 80% of the overall collection. Further space is needed for donations and civic acquisitions.

There's a sense of the endless warehouse of *Raiders of the Lost Ark* when visiting the Centre, with aisle after aisle of ceiling-high storage racks populating the colossal interior space, all occupied by a bewildering array of curiosities. The ground floor is characterised by science and industry, as those tend to be the larger and heavier objects. Familiar vehicles of yesteryear line up across from cast iron and electrical machinery of mysterious utility. Further up the racks, taxidermied representatives of the natural history collections can be glimpsed. Elsewhere, shelves and racks of vintage toys, signs, clothes and obsolete domestic appliances comprise a collective civic attic for the city.

The collection is ever growing: before the demolition of landmark buildings such as the large HP factory, the museum team quietly removed significant artefacts of city identity. More recently the team acquired windows, tiles and mirrors from the Eagle and Tun pub, noted for its associations with the band UB40 but since demolished.

Outside in the yard are the lost statues, fountains and crated public sculptures from years gone by. You may see the occasional caption, but this is an almost wholly uncurated experience, and therein lies its appeal. Each visitor's experience is unique, as different objects pique their curiosity or rouse long-dormant memories.

Address Museum Collection Centre, 25 Dollman Street, Nechells, Birmingham B7 4RQ, www.birminghammuseums.org.uk | Getting there Train from New Street to Duddeston Rail; bus 14 to Duddeston Rail Station, then a five-minute walk | Hours Open several times a year but booking ahead via the website is essential | Tip Visit Harry Seager's 1958 sculpture *Youth*, which overlooks the roundabout at the end of Melvina Road and is perhaps the city's least-known example of modern art.

79 Netherton Tunnel

Canalside walk for cavers

This is a canal-side walk with two clear benefits: it won't rain, and you certainly won't get lost. However, you may get slightly damp, and despite being a straight line, the experience is curiously disorientating. Netherton Tunnel cuts one-and-a-half miles beneath Dudley, just to the east of the two landmark TV masts on Rowley Hills. The scale of the tunnel is a reminder of the power of canal companies at their industrial peak. Until 1820, cargo narrowboats had to queue for days to access the nearby Dudley Tunnel. Cutting a new tunnel through the hill over three years was the practical solution to the bottleneck, with room for two adjacent narrowboats, and a towpath on either side for horses to pull vessels loaded with coal, stone and iron.

Walking through the tunnel feels closer to caving than a leisurely canal-side stroll, so be prepared: wear waterproof boots, and bring a good torch, as there is no lighting within. Start at the Dudley Port end and ensure that you are on the right-hand side of the canal as you approach the tunnel mouth. The tunnel is completely dark after 100 meters, but the light at the end of the tunnel is visible from the first step inside.

Many remark on how near the other end seems, but this is an illusion: the light will appear to remain the same size until you are nearly at the other end.

There are a few sections of flooded path that you can walk through easily with good boots or you can use the side railing to edge past the larger puddles. Along the way, several 'pepper pot' air vents drip eerily into the canal waters, and you'll see many white stone stalactites rippling down the brick inverts. Rusted iron markers chart your progress in units of five chains (20 meters). With the aid of your torch, you might also spot tench and carp in the murky waters. After an hour, you'll emerge into daylight at the picturesque Windmill End.

Address Entrance to tunnel on Dudley Canal, Tipton B69 | **Getting there** Train to Dudley Port, then follow Birmingham Canal on to Dudley Canal | **Tip** The tunnel takes you directly to Cobb's Engine House, a well-preserved brick structure originally a pumping station, built in 1831 to pump water from the nearby mines.

80 New Street Signal Box
Zigzagging concrete defies the bulldozers

Birmingham has a reputation for being the UK's concrete capital. After the heavy bombing sustained during the Second World War, the city rebuilt itself anew, using robust materials, and in a style that clearly spoke of resilience. New Street Signal Box dates from 1964, and is a striking example of this bold architecture. It is also a rare instance of one of the city's 20th-century buildings being awarded listed status.

Whatever your take is on the New Brutalist movement of the 1950s and 1960s, there were certainly some playful and genuinely new creations. For a decade in Birmingham, the style captured the character of the shell-shocked city, which opted not to simply rebuild its many Victorian losses. Since the beginning of the 20th century, many of those key buildings have been lost to the city's own eager revisionism. Seen from street level, it is less obvious that the signal box is a five-storey tower, rising through the city from track level. Its crinkle-cut, concrete fabric was intended by the architects Bicknell & Hamilton to resemble an electrical transformer, and a non-functional pulley on the Brunel Street corner signals 'industrial'. An array of several smaller corrugated modules accompany the main structure at ground level, and can be spotted from a departing train window.

The signal box wasn't designed as a public building, so getting a sense of its asymmetric, multi-level whole can be challenging. For the pedestrian, the best vantage point from which to see the entire building is the rear of the car park on Swallow Street, being careful if you need to step on the barrier. You may need to walk around the block to appreciate it fully, and indeed, the zig-zagging wall that runs along Navigation Street and up Hill Street should be seen as an extension of the same building. The wall's pebble-dashed coating hints at Birmingham's eternal longing for the seaside.

Address Brunel Street, Birmingham B5 4AD | Getting there Train to New Street or tram to Grand Central | Tip More listed 1960s Modernism can be glimpsed on the first floor of the Zara store beneath the Rotunda at 148 New Street. John Poole's richly textured Ciment Fondu mosaic, originally created for Lloyds Bank, still curves round the inner core of the tower behind the clothes racks.

81 New St Station Cladding

A distorted reflection of a city

In 2015, New Street Station underwent a radical revamp. The drab design urgently needed some zing, but no one was expecting the solution presented by the architecture firm AZPML. The original railway tracks and structure of the station were left intact, but the entire concrete exterior was veiled in a patchwork of warped, reflective, steel panels. Architecturally, it was like a practical but dated grey suit being replaced by a glitzy, lamé cabaret outfit.

The architects' express intention was to offer a new perception of the urban setting by reflecting areas of the townscape, the distortion representing the dynamic movement of a busy transport hub. It was a witty solution to a nearly impossible brief – how to blend in with the surrounding buildings – as this part of town is truly Birmingham at its most fragmented. The hall of mirrors literally reflects this aspect of the city's nature.

Exiting the station via 1000 Trades Square brings you to the brick back-end of the Odeon Cinema. It's an important company in the city's history, but this is the side that no one was meant to see. The jumbled postmodernism of the Bullring and the dramatic slabs of the Brutalist Midland Red bus station are dominated by the presence of the cylindrical tower of the Rotunda, once Birmingham's most distinctive landmark. That title is now being challenged by the station's mirror cladding. It is certainly one of the city's most photographed features, as tourists and locals spot themselves amongst the distortions. TV shows use the rippling backdrop to convey that the action has now moved to Birmingham.

The craggy elevations feature caverns, overhangs and headwalls more reminiscent of a mountainside than of a building. Three large, elliptical LED screens open in the facade's fabric, like Eyes of Sauron. Circle the station on foot to let the full impact of this coruscating drama unfold.

Address Station Street, Birmingham B2 4QA | Getting there Buses to the city centre and trains to New Street | Tip Cherry Reds is the city's favourite café bar with craft ales, cakes, coffee and cuisine in four eccentric rooms over two floors and outside seating (www.cherryreds.com, +44(0)121 643 5716).

82 Oak House

A 17th-century wealthy yeoman farmer's house

Oak House is a large and well-preserved 17th-century building that tells of an early industrial success story. It was built in the 1620s, with the Turton family – John, Elizabeth and their five children – in residence from 1634. This Puritan family were farmers and nailmakers by trade. The farmland around Oak House supported crops, livestock, hives and a kitchen garden.

The family fortune grew as they increased production of nails and blades, and this was reflected in alterations to the house. Stables were added, and the towering belvedere afforded the Turtons a finer view of the area. The distinctive vertical beams that give the house its striped appearance, characteristic of the Midlands, survived the alterations, but the back of the house is brick-faced in the Flemish tradition, then at the height of architectural fashion. Inside, a feature staircase was added with distinctive carved balusters, featuring hearts and diamonds and reminiscent of the folkcraft 'love spoons' popular at the time. Taper marks can be seen in some places around the house, apotropaic burns made to protect against lightning and fire. Elsewhere on the timbers are carpenters' marks, symbols that worked as practical assembly guides.

By Victorian times, Oak House had become a museum. A key figure from the time was teacher, diarist and explorer Helen Caddick, who wrote extensively about her travels to Palestine, China, Burma and Africa. The clothes, stuffed animals and artefacts she returned with once populated the museum, and can be seen on open days, when other rooms in the house become accessible. By the 1950s, the museum became a representation of a historic house, with the period furniture and reconstructed interiors on display today. The extensive gardens are family-friendly, while maintaining a sense of the 17th century. Wild flowers are encouraged, and recent summers have seen several spikes of bee orchids.

Address Oak Road, West Bromwich B70 8HJ, +44 (0)121 553 0759, www.sandwell.gov.uk |
Getting there Tram to Lodge Road, then a five-minute walk; bus 74 to West Bromwich
Bus Station, then an eight-minute walk | **Hours** Tue–Thu 11am–3.30pm, Sat & Sun
11am–2pm | **Tip** Lynpurl Well, once the main water supply for West Bromwich, still
bubbles up from an alcove in front of 58 Stoney Lane; unfortunately, the free-flowing waters
have made the stone plaque unreadable, and weeds abundant.

83　Old Joe

AKA The Joseph Chamberlain Memorial Clock Tower

It's that Italian influence again. The Joseph Chamberlain Memorial Tower widely signals the University's presence across south Birmingham. The monumental campanile pays tribute to Joseph Chamberlain, the influential Victorian statesman who started out as a screw manufacturer, then became Mayor, and later Member of Parliament for Birmingham. While holidaying in Italy, he saw the imposing campanile of Torre del Mangia in Siena, and decided that was right for the new university. It was built in 1905 by Aston Webb and Ingress Bell, in the later years of Chamberlain's life. Although he lived a few miles away in Kings Heath, the clock tower would have been visible from his home (you can test this in Highbury Park), and the bell tower's chimes carry a surprising distance.

Old Joe, as the tower is affectionately known, demonstrates the adventures that can be had with red brick. Its vertical flutes and striking stone stripes have timeless appeal, and are mirrored in the surrounding buildings. The tower can appear unexpectedly on the horizon, even from much more remote parts of the city, as a sight line opens up between buildings and trees. The view from Rookery Road in Selly Oak is recommended, where the campanile and saucer domes of the university campus appear in the middle-distance like an exotic citadel. Viewed from the staircase at the side of the Bramhall Music Building, the entire height of the clock tower is neatly framed by an aperture in the architecture.

The clock tower is free standing, and an archway at the base allows you to walk directly beneath it. Many claim that Old Joe is the world's tallest campanile; however, elsewhere in Italy is the Mortegliano free-standing bell tower, which is taller by *un po'* – just a little. As with the proud Birmingham boast 'more canals than Venice', perhaps the humble lesson here is that we should measure quality, not quantity.

Address Chancellor's Court, University of Birmingham Edgbaston, Birmingham B15 2TT |
Getting there Train from New Street to University, then a five-minute walk; bus 62 or 63 to
Bournbrook Road | Tip The Bramall Music Building in Chancellor Court hosts diverse and
regular concerts, exhibitions, lectures and workshops.

84 Orange Chips
Black Country gold

How do you sauce your chip? The various UK regions treat their fried potatoes differently. In the north of England you might be offered gravy, in the south tomato ketchup, and cheesy chips in Scotland – to the delight or bafflement of those from outside the area. The orange chip is the West Midlands' own regional contribution to chip shop cuisine. It's a black country speciality that is beginning to appear in Birmingham areas bordering the Black Country, and is a coating rather than a condiment.

There's no way around it: the mysterious orange tincture comes not from a secret blend of herbs and spices, but from orange food colouring. However, the batter has its own piquant ingredients which make the battered coating a unique experience. Recipes vary from shop to shop, with many owners priding themselves on keeping a family recipe a secret. However, some ingredients that can regularly be tasted in the mix include paprika, turmeric, garlic powder, salt and black pepper, with sparkling water added for texture.

The true secret of buying deep-fried chips is in the timing of your visit. They are fresher, fluffier and crunchier straight from the frier, and you might prefer to avoid those that may have been resting in oil during a lull in trade (although the soggy chip does have its own fans). Arrive soon after opening time to catch them at their crispiest, or perhaps a fresh fry around supper time.

Some outlets have specific days of the week on which orange chips are available, alternating with unbattered. Tracing the origins of the orange chip is to descend into legend. Many outlets claim theirs to be the original, while others claim to be the best. Certainly there was an expansion in popularity in the 1990s, and that's when many remember their first encounter with the vivid snack but some make claims for far earlier. An ardent debate is part of the tradition.

Address 635 Bearwood Road, Bearwood B66 4BL | Getting there Bus 9 or 126 to Lordswood Road | Hours Mon–Sat noon–9.30pm | Tip Orange chips are common and widespread across the Black Country but nearer to Birmingham city centre is The Sailors, their orange anchor logo being the clue to their taste in chips. Take your chips to nearby Lightwoods Park, expansive greenery and the setting for the 18th-century Lightwoods House.

85___Outside-In

Ikon Gallery's spy glass

Oliver Beer's 'Outside-In' sculpture replaces a pane of Ikon Gallery's front-facing window, positioned several feet off the ground, and over-looking the outside terrace of Yorks café. On the face of it, this work resembles the pontil mark or 'bullseye' sometimes seen on old window panes, that being the scar of the glass-making process, as it is spun around a central rod. However, far from being a defective pane, this is an artwork designed by Beer and made the respected French crystal works Hermés.

The work, which appeared in 2013, forms part of a collection of permanent but discrete installations around the gallery. The node extends several inches into the building, leaving a delicate but pre-cise tube for gallery visitors to make use of, should they notice it. The location is strategic: gently bringing your ear to the tube's opening reveals that it functions as an ear trumpet, capturing the everyday sounds of Oozell's Square as effectively as a microphone. You might be surprised to catch snippets of conversation as people pass by, or even listen in on entire discourses of those seated within the café, as they enjoy a coffee – or perhaps a glass of beer. The exercise is a care-ful balance of cautious involvement, then discreet withdrawal from the private lives of others.

As a piece of surveillance equipment, this device certainly has its drawbacks: it's not easy to hear and see people at the same time, and the subterfuge is highly visible to anyone facing the window out-side – although practical espionage was never the intention of the work. Instead 'Outside-In' may prompt meditations on the nature and function of windows, where the 'outside' of a building begins and ends, as well as thoughts about the increasing presence of surveillance systems in our lives. You might also like to reflect on your complicity in the illicit activity of eavesdropping. In a gesture of affinity with the olde worlde, the tube is bunged shut at night with a large cork.

Address 1 Oozells Square, Brindleyplace, Birmingham B1 2HS, +44 (0)121 248 0708, www.ikon-gallery.org | **Getting there** Tram to Brindleyplace, then a five-minute walk; bus to Broad Street | **Hours** Tue – Sun 11am – 4pm | **Tip** Ikon Gallery's shop is a superior hoard of artistically-inclined jewellery, T-shirts, prints, posters, magazines and books.

86 _ Perrott's Folly

Inscrutable tower from the 18th century

Rising 96 feet above the surrounding suburbs of Ladywood, Perrott's Folly has long piqued the curiosity and imagination of its neighbours. The brick tower is seven storeys high, features many windows of different shapes, and has an octagonal cross-section with a round stair core added to one side. The observation deck at the top features defensive crenellations.

The tower was previously known as The Monument (a nearby road acknowledges this) and also as The Observatory. Stories down the years suggest a variety of rather unlikely explanations: the occupant built it to spy on his wife, or to see her grave in over-the-horizon Belbroughton, or perhaps as a viewing platform for a wealthy land owner. The folly's name comes from John Perrott, son of a rich family who lived at Bell Hall in Belbroughton, Worcester. Perrott owned land in Birmingham, and in 1758 built the tower near his house, which would then have been deep in the countryside and well away from the noise of the town.

Several clues suggest the tower's original purpose. The pointed windows represent a voguish revival of the Gothic style, perhaps prompted by Horace Walpole's ostentatious villa Strawberry Hill. Individual rooms have fireplaces and ornately moulded plaster, so were intended to be occupied. The battlements are merely decorative, the architect evoking a feudal past that was long over by the 18th century. This could well have been the clubhouse and hunting lodge for Perrott to show off his land and property to his friends and company.

By the 1880s, the tower was being used for weather observations by the glass-maker and meteorologist Abraham Follet Osler, and is still being used by the University of Birmingham for this purpose today. The tower has recently been bought by an arts organisation, which plans to make it open to the public, and a greater focus of the community.

Address 44 Waterworks Road, Ladywood, Birmingham B16 9AL, www.refuturecollective.com | **Getting there** Bus 9, 10, 13 or 126 to the Ivy Bush, then a five-minute walk | **Tip** Further down Waterworks Street is another eccentric tower, this one being the chimney of the pumping station, disguised in 1870 as an Italianate campanile to appease its wealthy Edgbaston neighbours. One of these was the young J R R Tolkien, whose works famously feature two towers as well as an inn named the Ivy Bush.

87 Piccadilly Arcade

Elegant arcade hides a secret

A stroll down Piccadilly Arcade may suggest that it is nothing more than an attractive and ornate passageway with a selection of independent shops and – if you spot them – some curious frescos added at a later date. You may regard the arcade as a rare moment of chancing upon some original features in a constantly developing city. The arcade's secret is that it used to be a cinema dating back to the silent era, and that the arcade and shopfronts were all installed later.

The Picture House was opened in 1910 to an audience hungry for cinema, which was then in its infancy. The cinema lived its short life entirely within the silent era, closing by 1926. Unlike the fleapits of the suburbs, it was a deluxe experience, with cafés and richly decorated interiors. The ornate front elevation, complete with cherubs and Baroque turrets, betrays nothing of the building's function, although cinemas would soon begin to assume their own distinctive style (see ch. 103 for the Odeon story). However, the cinema's narrow footprint didn't allow for expansion, and in 1926 developers opened another, larger cinema across town in order to satisfy audience demand, and closed the picture house.

The shape of the structure was ideal for an arcade. If, when walking through, the floor seems a little steep, this is because you're walking down the rake of the stalls' floor line. It is interesting to see how different retailers have responded to the problem of placing a small bench outside their unit on the slope. During an overhaul in 1989, Paul Maxfield's frescos were added along the arcade's ceiling panels. They unfold sequentially and surreally, like a silent short film before the main feature. The title *A Life In The Year Of The Chinchillas* only makes the parachutist's descent through the seasons, amongst urban skyscapes peppered with coded references and *memento mori*, even more intriguing.

Address Piccadilly Arcade, New Street, Birmingham B2 4EU | **Getting there** Train to New Street; tram to Grand Central | **Hours** The arcade is accessible Mon–Sat 7am–7pm, Sun 11am–5pm | **Tip** Another early, former cinema building can be found on John Bright Street. The pink and cream building now occupied by a shisha lounge was once The Futurist, the first cinema in the city to screen 'talkies'.

88 Pillbox

Stirchley's lost bunker

The concrete cylinder standing on the far side of the Birmingham and Worcester canal as it passes through Stirchley defends an intriguing secret. If anyone notices the structure tucked between a spreading tree and a large metal shed, they would assume it to be a chimney, as this is an industrial stretch of the canal. However, this is in fact a pillbox dating back to the Second World War: a reinforced guard post positioned as a defensive measure against an attacking enemy. It incorporates a lookout post, making this a rare and important piece of military history, and which in 2018 was listed for its architectural interest. So what is this doing alongside a canal in Birmingham?

The pillbox was constructed around 1940 next to Guest, Keen and Nettlefolds Ltd, a screw manufacturer that expanded into the production of Spitfires, parts for tanks, and steel helmets, as a result of which it became a prime target for enemy bombing. Many factories made this transition, and being an industrial city, Birmingham endured regular air raids. Many canals, bridges and rivers were also defended in this way, but the structures were demolished in peacetime when they obstructed roads and footpaths; those that were less obstructive survived.

The lower section is a Croft pillbox produced by the Croft Granite, Brick and Concrete Company of Leicester. The loopholes or gun embrasures are clearly visible once you know what they are. The structure above was cemented on to the pillbox and was probably a fire watch tower. Fire watchers manned roofs of buildings to look out for incendiary bombs or tackle fires that started until the fire brigade arrived. If an attack on the factory was direct, the pillbox allowed the fire watcher to take cover. The best time to visit the pillbox is during autumn and winter, when the adjacent tree has shed its leaves, allowing a better view.

Address Opposite Waterside Business Park, 1649 Pershore Road, Kings Norton B30 3DR | **Getting there** Bus 45 or 47 to Stirchley and join the towpath at Lifford Lane; train to Bournville, then a 10-minute walk | **Tip** Follow the towpaths to Tunnel Lane to visit Lifford Reservoir, and to get a glimpse of the 17th-century Lifford Hall; tranquillity amongst the noise of the mineral works and recycling centre.

89 Prefabs

Long live temporary housing!

Prefab housing in the UK was a popular solution to the problem of housing lost to bombing during the Second World War. Individual houses, parts of streets or sometimes entire estates would be replaced by compact, prefabricated and quick-to-assemble bungalows. What was intended to be a temporary living solution for perhaps 10 years or so became a permanent and desirable home for many.

Wake Green Road in Hall Green features a row of 17 surviving prefabs of the Phoenix type from 1945, several of which are still proudly occupied. One recurring belief is that temporary prefab living was basic, but the fittings that came as standard were better than most of the neighbours', featuring very modern fitted kitchens, central heating and indoor toilets. Those on Wake Green Road have a small front lawn and plenty of green space at the back for growing flowers, fruit and vegetables. There was a strong sense of community amongst the prefabs: families with young children were the first to be rehoused here, and most households would have experienced similar disasters, helping each other through their new situations well into peace time. Perhaps part of the bungalows' enduring appeal comes from their similarity to the popular holiday chalet camps provided by Butlin's, which had their origins in the 1930s.

Materials used for prefabs included wood, metal and concrete. Those at Wake Green Road are made from uniform magnolia asbestos panels, which led to many UK prefabs being hastily demolished. However, in 1998 the city council made the unexpected decision to list 16 of the 17 prefabs, recognising the importance of the houses in the city's architectural story. More wartime prefabs still stand at Austin Village (see ch. 8), built from kits during the First World War, when the car factory at Longbridge took on more workers to build military vehicles.

Address 395–427 Wake Green Road, Birmingham B13 0BG | Getting there Bus 2 or 3, then transfer to bus 11A to Wake Green Road | Tip Behind the prefabs is the John Morris Jones Walkway, named after the local historian who keenly researched the 18th-century watermill Sarehole Mill, where this pastoral riverside path leads.

90 Provide
Unapologetically Brummie design

Anyone seeking Birmingham souvenirs during their visit to the city may well come away empty-handed. The city has successively scaled back its Tourist Information Centres, with the New Street kiosk closing in 2012, and just a few tea towels, post cards and remaindered history tomes at the Library of Birmingham's information desk. For those in the know, the savvy option is to shop at Provide, which has for the last decade built up a graphic-focussed collection of products aimed at more discerning citizens.

At its heart, Provide responds to a city which regularly downplays its cultural importance, pinning it down with a direct wit and a clear and recognisable look. Bold, contemporary graphics embrace places and sayings unique to Birmingham, sometimes paying a cheeky but affectionate tribute to the familar branding of Birmingham companies and organisations. The popularity of the products has renewed confidence in the locations, sayings and tropes usually only known to locals. Many products are collaborations with other like-minded artists and designers, which bear their style but are unmistakably 'Provide'. The omnipresent 'Alright Bab?' design, originally painted by a local sign-writer, was a breakthrough moment, appearing on mugs, hats and slipmats (note: don't look here for tea towels, fridge magnets or other moribund kitchenalia). The bold and brutal architecture of the 1960s regularly features in Provide's range. Its most sought-after product is the limited edition Brum Box, which appears several times a year, housing a T-shirt, original print and mystery gift.

In 2017 the Provide shop went online, but products can still be spotted in temporary locations, most recently in Selfridges and the Ikon Gallery. Visitors and residents can shop online and then collect their goods directly from Provide's studio, and urgent orders can even be express-shipped to your hotel.

Address 201 Jubilee Trade Centre, Pershore Street, Birmingham B5 6ND,
+44 (0)121 769 2981, www.providebirmingham.com and www.brumbox.co.uk | Getting
there Train to New Street, then a six-minute walk | Hours Online orders can be collected on
weekdays – phone ahead to confirm | Tip The Quarter Horse Café & Roastery is perhaps the
city's most specialist coffee outlet, roasting fresh beans daily, offering coffee masterclasses, and
selling a wide selection of coffee-themed merchandise (88–90 Bristol Street).

91 Ristorante Caffe' Gustami

Authentic Italian cuisine in a humble setting

The Tolkien-sounding Twin Towers shopping plaza on King Edwards Road – in characteristically dry Brummie humour – takes its name from the two blocks of flats overlooking it. The modest precinct showcases Birmingham's super-diverse culture, with the Blessing Market (a Mwana Congo food store) neighbouring Grillo's Halal Peri-Peri takeaway. Next door to Pablo's Jamaican Laundry & Dry Cleaners is Ristorante Caffe' Gustami, which represents the best of the city's Italian restaurants.

The establishment deliberately avoids the random passing trade of the city centre and has earned a word-of-mouth reputation for serving authentic, quality homemade food for the more discerning diner. Note that Gustami (Italian for 'savour me') doesn't advertise, but it is often fully booked, so be sure to reserve ahead. Please also note that there are two King Edward Roads in close proximity. Diners visit from all over Birmingham and beyond.

Gustami was recently taken over from the original restaurateur Shawky El Sayed – a former chef to Luciano Pavarotti – by Raffaele, Silvio and Giovanni. Raffaele, native of Milan, spent twenty years working in Birmingham's various Italian restaurants before settling into his own authentic trattoria. Almost all the ingredients here are sourced from Italy, wines are specially selected and imported, and, unlike many restaurants, the food is prepared from scratch in the kitchen. Fresh sage and other herbs are grown in Raffaele's garden.

A generous specials menu is always on offer, with the chef's own tweaks on traditional dishes. Don't look for spurious Italian offerings like spaghetti Bolognese or garlic bread here! Raffaele's signature dish is tortelloni, acknowledging his grandmother's cooking in Bologna. Former chef Shawky's creation, the mezzaluna (or half-moon) pasta, with a filling dependent on the season, still lives on in the ever-changing menu.

Address 4 King Edwards Road, Birmingham B1 2PZ, +44 (0)121 454 5922, www.ristorantecaffegustami.uk | Getting there Bus 82, 87 or 89 to Spring Hill Island | Hours Mon–Thu noon–10pm, Fri & Sat noon–11pm, Sun noon–5pm | Tip Modernists can find a lesser-known panel by John Poole on the Ledbury Close side of Ladywood Health and Community Centre (222 St Vincent Street West).

92___The Roundhouse
Horseshoe-shaped corporation stables

For years, Birmingham residents have been bamboozled by the curious Martello tower-like structure on the Birmingham Canal Old Line. Standing at the far end of a canal-side pub's courtyard, many have imagined its high curved walls to be the defensive measure of a fortress or even an old prison. Now, thanks to a joint venture between the National Trust and Canal and River Trust, the truth regarding the origins of this mysterious edifice can be revealed.

The Roundhouse is the modern name for the Sheepcote Street Corporation Depot. The city has a long tradition of producing landmark curvaceous buildings such as the Rotunda and Selfridges, and perhaps this all began in 1873, with W H Ward's solution for corporation stables and warehouses. In pre-car Birmingham, horses provided vehicle pulling power, and this is where the horses rested after a hard day's work.

Venture to the far side of the Distillery's courtyard, and you'll find a tunnel leading to the inner parts of the depot. The interior yard is lined with cobbles – more properly called setts – sourced from Rowley quarry (see ch. 93). The ring is not quite complete: paired Gothic lodges act as gatehouses, and the circle is only completed when the gates are closed. There are conflicting theories to explain the unusual shape. Was this an experimental turning circle for loading and unloading the horses' carts and to keep traffic flowing? Or is this in fact a giant horseshoe? Perhaps both are true. It's delightful to think that the pragmatic industrialists still had time for whimsy.

The Roundhouse's new role is as a hub for canal and waterway exploration by foot, cycle and kayak – currently lacking in the city, and welcome alternatives to the city's petrol-powered dominance. A café, gallery, kayaking and office space for the National Trust are all recent additions to the newly opened Roundhouse.

Address The Roundhouse, 1 Sheepcote Street, Birmingham B16 8AE, www.RoundhouseBirmingham.org.uk | **Getting there** A short stroll along the tow path from Brindleyplace; bus 24 to NIA | **Hours** Daily 10am–5pm | **Tip** The Distillery next door is another converted Victorian warehouse, now a working gin distillery and eatery with excellent canal-side seating. The copper pot still used for brewing the gin resembles a Victorian time machine (www.thedistillerybirmingham.co.uk).

93 Rowley Hills

Overlooked viewpoint in reclaimed quarry

Birmingham is located upon rather flat terrain, so you may need to leave the city boundaries to find a good view of the area. Lickey Hills is Birmingham's go-to country park, but Rowley Hills is nearer to the city centre and has great views of Cannock Chase, Clent and Clee Hills, with the Birmingham skyline in the distance. This is as high as it gets in the West Midlands.

Four hills make up the Rowley Hills: Bury Hill, Portway Hill, Darby's Hill and – topped with the imposing TV and radio towers – Turner's Hill. After a steep ascent through Bury Hill Park and what must be the West Midlands' highest football pitch, the terrain levels off, with footpaths criss-crossing the grassland. Wild flowers are plentiful, with honeysuckle, goat's beard, peach-leaved bellflower and, though you may need to visit regularly to spot them, bee orchids. Several species of butterfly, as well as kestrels and buzzards, are also regular visitors.

The land of Rowley Hills was formerly what locals might call 'the Quacks' or quarries. Parts were active until 2008, but have been landscaped for leisure use in recent years. Rowley Rag was quarried here – a tough stone that Birmingham used for kerbs and cobbles (or rather 'setts') – and it turns up around the area in dry stone walls marking field boundaries. The Romans also used it for their road construction. See the Roundhouse (ch. 92) for info on where the stone was unloaded to be broken up.

The presence of the quarry is still apparent under the grasslands, with the stepped rises still visible. Rowley Rag is volcanic basalt, as seen at The Giant's Causeway in Northern Ireland, and the same hexagonal pillars can be discerned in the open sections of the quarry on Turner's Hill. Beneath the quarries were two extensive coal mines, Alston and Lye Cross, making this beautiful nature reserve a truly industrial destination.

Address Wolverhampton Road, Oldbury B69 2BJ, www.friendsofrowleyhills.org | Getting there Bus 126 to Florence Road | Tip You can extend your rural ramble through to Netherton. The footpath cuts across Dudley Golf Club to reach Warrens Hall and Bumble Hole nature reserves. Refreshments at the excellent Black Country pub Ma Pardoe's – otherwise known as The Old Swan Inn – at 87 Halesowen Road, Netherton, Dudley.

94 Rowton House

Affordable city living for Victorian workers

Guests at the Rowton Hotel may sometimes ask the question 'But what did it used to be?' The huge, distinctive, red brick building has a defensive, fortified feel, and over the years some have variously guessed workhouse, prison or even asylum. The answer is that the building was actually built as a hotel, or rather a high-end hostel, intended to provide cheap, hygienic lodging for men arriving in the city to work.

It was one of seven 'Rowton Houses' introduced as a measure to improve the lives of city-dwelling workers by the Victorian philanthropist Lord Rowton, the others all being in London. They were designed along similar lines by architect Harry Bell Measures, who went on to design military barracks. His style conveyed a sense of resilience, with six-storey towers at the corners, each surrounded by terracotta dragons, wings outstretched and clutching a shield to their chests. The unusual dimensions of the windows suggest the loopholes of a castle. A pair of cherubim are shown working at the forge in the panels above the porch and could be a sly reference to the child workers of the industrial revolution, who started work as young as eight.

Rowton House had a lot to offer guests for their nightly sixpence. Guests had their own private room with window, chamber pot, clean sheets daily, and a horsehair mattress (a step up in luxury from grain husks). There was a dining room, a reading room with 300 books, a smoking room with newspapers and games, a writing room (most men were away from their families), washrooms, barbers and tailors. Some rooms, known as 'specials', gave guests conditions closer to those of a hotel. In his *Down and Out in Paris and London*, George Orwell wrote about the Rowton Houses of the early 1930s, praising them as being the best of available hostel accommodation options, but also lamented their strictness and numerous rules.

Address 145 Alcester Street, Birmingham B12 0PJ | Getting there Bus 50 to Alcester Street | Tip Behind the Rowton Hotel is St Anne's Hostel, occupying the former Digbeth Police Station. Ken Loach's TV play about homelessness *Cathy Come Home* features some scenes filmed at the hostel (www.stannesbirmingham.org.uk).

95 St Basil's Church

An Italian touch in deepest Digbeth

St Basil's church offers a ray of light in unlikely surroundings, sandwiched as it is between an empty industrial shed and a limousine hire service. Its modest scale and setting means it can easily be missed, and the encounter has a sense of the pastoral Italian village about it.

Like many plots in Digbeth, the compact front elevation hides the full extent of the building's cruciform plan. The church, which dates from 1911, showcases the creative possibilities of brick, and absolutely transforms the material from its utilitarian associations. The architect, Arthur Stansfield Dixon, was the founder of the Birmingham Guild of Handicraft, and this is perhaps Birmingham's finest instance of Arts and Crafts style. Heath Mill Lane has plenty of factories with Romanesque arched windows, so those of St Basil fit in well, though here the infill is treated more like stained glass than brick. Diamond patterns echo the actual glass windows, and there are several shades of brick in use. The blue engineering bricks, fired to a higher temperature and more robust, are also seen in the nearby railway viaducts, which themselves have Romanesque overtones in their arches. The round, projecting baptistry also features this playful use of brick, and may remind some of Battenberg cake. A close look at the bricks themselves reveals a secondary pattern, which represents evidence of how the clay bricks were stacked in the kiln.

At ground level, cobbles decorate the paved area leading up to the entrances. The bellcote is now missing its bell, but still hints at the tranquil piazza, and the curved, 'double Roman' roof tiles complete the sense of being transported to a remote, idyllic setting. St Basil was deconsecrated in 1978, and is now occupied by a youth homelessness charity named after the church, meaning the retained interior is no longer accessible to the public.

Address 120 Heath Mill Lane, Digbeth, Birmingham B9 4AX | Getting there 12-minute walk from the city centre or bus 97 to Heath Mill Lane | Tip A now-disused chapel on High Street, Deritend further evokes the spirit of Little Italy, built in 1913 after the 7th-century San Giorgio in Velabro, Rome.

96 St Thomas' Garden

War and Peace between the ring roads

In a surprisingly calm spot sandwiched between the Inner and Middle Ring Road is The Peace Garden, presided over by all that remains of St Thomas' church. The church was hit by enemy bombing on the night of 11 December, 1940, in an air raid that lasted 13 hours, and was the heaviest attack of the Birmingham Blitz. Blast damage is still visible in the lower stonework. Only the tower and portico survived, and – like Coventry, whose cathedral had been largely destroyed a few weeks earlier – the remains were left standing as a permanent memorial to the losses of the Second World War. Burials were relocated from the churchyard to Warstone Lane Cemetery, and the rubble cleared to form a public garden.

In 1989, the colonnade along the north side of the garden was relocated stone by stone from Centenary Square, being a 1926 memorial to the First World War. In 1995, the grounds were restyled as the current Peace Garden to commemorate the 50th anniversary of the end of the Second World War, and it is now a memorial to all those who have died in armed conflict. The gardens display international messages of peace from Sweden, Sicily, Milan and Russia, and memorials from organisations such as British Nuclear Veterans, CND and the Humanists. The perimeter railings were created by Anuradha Patel, and feature elephants, whales, horses, doves and people in cut-out silhouettes. Bombs transform, Escher-like, into fish and doves as you walk around the fence (be careful which direction you choose to walk round in). Benches around the Peace Garden have forked-tailed snakes as supports, a reminder of the Garden of Eden.

In 1998, Birmingham hosted the 24th G8 summit, and the world leaders each planted a tree in the garden to represent their nation. Tony Blair planted an English Oak, Helmut Kohl a Kaiser Linden, Boris Yeltsin a Silver Birch, and Bill Clinton planted a California Redwood.

Address Holloway Head, Birmingham B15 1LZ, www.hallofmemory.co.uk | Getting there Bus 80, X 21 Platinum or X 22 Platinum to Granville Street | Hours Daily 10am–5pm | Tip At 41 Gas Street is the former Gas Retort House of 1822, originally used to extract gas from coal for municipal use, and which in recent years has functioned as a church. Despite the street's name, it went unnoticed until 1992.

97 Shard End Griffins
Six stone sentinels keep guard in Shard End

This is a discovery few will make by chance, and one that only the city's keenest urban adventurers are likely to know about. These monumental grotesques are intimately familiar to the families living on Horne Way, a pedestrian walkway that cuts through the bungalows in this green part of Shard End. Six stone griffins, standing in three pairs and facing each other, guard the lime tree-lined avenue. The squawks of parakeets permanently settled in the surrounding trees give the encounter with the six sentinels an Indiana Jones feel, the suggestions of remains from a lost civilisation.

The fantastic animals squat nobly, and proudly push out their feathered chests and weathered features. All are similar in scale – just higher than the tallest human likely to visit – but each griffin's head is subtly different, with either birdlike or lionlike characteristics, and none are quite symmetrical. Paws and claws are visible on some, while others disappear beneath the ground. The sculptures are made from three sections of roughly rendered stone, and have occasional touches of soot, which hint at their more metropolitan origins. Their heads and backs are mossy, and some have attracted ivy from nearby gardens. Repairs have been made to their knees and wingtips, after generations of playful clambering by local children. But where did they come from and how did they get here?

Between 1885 and 1923, they topped Lewis's department store on the corner of Corporation Street and Bull Street, three on each side. They were salvaged when the building was demolished, next appearing outside a scout hut in Shard End. When the hut was demolished to make way for housing in the 1970s, the griffins remained. Local folklore suggests the sculptures were a gift to Birmingham from the Tsar of Russia. If true, their setting in a department store would have been unusual, but it would explain the desire to keep the sculptures intact.

Address Horne Way, Birmingham B34 7SW | Getting there Bus 95 to Yorkswood Scout Camp | Tip Green and pleasant surroundings can be found alongside the river Cole at Kingfisher Country Park, accessible from Packington Avenue.

98 Shri Venkateswara Temple
Beautiful Hindu temple complex

The presence of the world's oldest religion is signalled by the intricately ornate design of the towering vimana above Shri Venkateswara Temple, transcending its urban, industrial setting between Oldbury and Tipton. The ancient Hindu design belies the temple's recent construction, opening in 2006. Since then, the temple has welcomed visitors and worshippers from all around the West Midlands, the UK and even further afield.

Venkateshwara is one of the forms of the Hindu god Vishnu, named after the Venkata hill in Andhra Pradesh, South India. Accordingly, this temple is located near a hill (Rowley Hills – see ch. 93) and as with an Indian temple, it is located near water – the river Tame and the Gower branch canal – notionally to allow baptisms. The temple welcomes all faiths; visitors may walk the grounds, enter the main Pooja hall (phones and shoes off), or devotees can attend a ceremony, bookable in advance. The Temple's website explains the code of conduct and the religious services offered. The five-storey tower in grey granite is the most visible aspect of the temple complex – a tough material intended to last centuries. Throughout the complex are carved and moulded peacocks, elephants and cobras of traditional Indian sacred design.

The main temple is complemented by the smaller towers of the surrounding temples and shrines. The yellow brick rotunda of Gandhi Peace Centre represents simplicity and the eternal, containing an exhibition of the life and work of Mahatma Gandhi. The community hall merges traditional and contemporary architecture and stages cultural events, social gatherings and weddings. In a pool, Krishna, the Hindu god of compassion and protection, reclines on the seven-headed serpent Adishesha, one of the primal beings of creation. Painted on the walkways between the shrines and annexes are many vividly depicted sacred designs.

Address Dudley Road East, Oldbury B69 3DU, +44 (0)121 544 2256,
www.venkateswara.org.uk | Getting there Train to Sandwell and Dudley, then a 22-minute
walk; bus 87 to Meadows School | Hours Mon–Fri 9am–1pm & 5–9pm, Sat, Sun &
Bank Holidays 9am–2.30pm & 4–9pm; closes 8.30pm Mar–Nov | Tip Follow the Gower
Branch Canal through to the rivers, pools and woodland of Sheepwash Nature Reserve,
Sheepwash Lane, Tipton.

99 Snow Hill Mosaic

Clues to Sherlock Holmes' Birmingham connection

When walking down the 17 steps from Snow Hill plaza, it's possible to entirely miss Oliver Budd's mosaic on the low curved walls to either side of the staircase. This mosaic depicts the history of Snow Hill railway station from Isambard Kingdom Brunel's Great Western Railway line to Paddington in 1847, through to the last days of steam in the late 1930s. The mosaic has an interesting history in itself, being a reproduction in miniature of the original by Oliver's father, Kenneth Budd, which once adorned a nearby subway underpass.

Kenneth had a keen eye for historical detail, and included several references to Birmingham figures as passengers in the train's carriages. On the left-hand panel, clearly recognisable despite their cubist renderings in miniature, are the seated profiles of Doctor Watson and Sherlock Holmes. Birmingham may not be the first city associated with Sir Arthur Conan Doyle's detective stories, but Budd was clearly aware of the creator's placement while a medical student at an Aston dispensing pharmacy, which took place between 1879 and 1882. A blue plaque on Aston Road North commemorates this.

Like Budd's mosaic, the Sherlock Holmes stories are scattered with clues to Birmingham characters and locations, the most notable being John Baskerville lending his name to Doyle's famous hound (see ch. 59). During Doyle's time in the city, Sherlock Street just south of the city centre would have been a busy and popular commercial destination. In the short story 'The Adventure of the Stockbroker's Clerk', Holmes and Watson travel from Euston to Birmingham to investigate a financial mystery, visiting an office at 126B Corporation Street. It is fascinating to piece together the clues Doyle left, with this last one revealing that Birmingham once had its own stock exchange, located in a building that still stands on Margaret Street.

Address Snow Hill Station, Colmore Row, Birmingham B3 2BJ; at the right of the station entrance, follow the steps down towards Colmore Circus Queensway | Getting there Short walk from the city centre | Tip Another carriage features an homage to *The Travelling Companions*, Augustus Egg's painting of 1862. The original is on permanent display in the Round Room of Birmingham Museum and Art Gallery, Chamberlain Square (reopening in 2024).

100 Spaghetti Junction

It's complicated

Spaghetti Junction could have emerged with a more romantic name. The original newspaper report described it as a 'cross between a plate of spaghetti and an unsuccessful attempt at a Staffordshire knot'. The spaghetti image stuck, however, and since 1971 hardly anybody calls it the Gravelly Hill Interchange. Most experience it by car and are gone within a minute, and although bolder pedestrians may visit on foot, safely away from any traffic, this can be a jarring experience, wholly unlike the milder waterway walks Birmingham has to offer.

Approach on foot along the Grand Union Canal towpath, and just past Saltley viaduct you will be walking in parallel with the river Rea: this is an exchange not only of roads and motorways, but also of canal, rail and river. Once you reach the interchange, you'll see the river Tame, which in another context would be a more tranquil encounter. The scale here is epic. A huge concrete colonnade supports the multi-level tangle of A roads, and although you won't see any vehicles, the ominous thunder of their passing is ever-present. The landscape seems unfinished, with piles of sand, scaffolding and hastily constructed barriers shoring up the river banks. Bridges from many eras, gas and electric lines and graffiti populate the discordant landscape, while electricity pylons fizz overhead. Amongst the urban constructs, however, it's also possible to see anglers and herons competing for fish.

Follow the towpath to the right along the Tame Valley canal for a rare moment of culture: a square aperture in the overpass illuminates a constantly evolving painted text work by the artist Bill Drummond, in place over 2014–2025. Drummond regards the location as the 'gates to the underworld'. A final towpath memorial completes the bleak picture: a tribute to Police Officer Michael Swindles, killed in the line of duty in 2004.

Address Tyburn Road, Birmingham B24 8NP | Getting there By car, M6 or A38(M); train or bus 65 or 67 to Gravelly Hill; on foot, follow the Birmingham & Fazeley Canal or Grand Union Canal towpath | Tip The beautiful interior of the Greek Orthodox Church of the Holy Trinity & St Luke at Magnet Centre, Park Approach B23 7SJ provides a glorious contrast to Spaghetti Junction (see www.holytrinityandstluke.org.uk for their monthly programme of services).

101 Stratford House

Ambrose and Bridget Rotton's farmstead

Stratford House is a familiar sight to passengers on the number 50 bus, but is rarely considered a destination in its own right. The building represents an intriguing side of Birmingham's earlier days. Very little of 17th-century Birmingham still stands (Aston Hall being the most visible example) but the facade of Stratford House gives a good indication of what a prosperous farmhouse of the day looked like. Today, only the facade, the heavy oak door and a few internal timbers are original, but the illusion of completeness from the front is convincing.

The facade shows two distinct and very fashionable designs of the day. The first floor timbers are arranged in a striking herringbone design, which used much more wood than was necessary, and created extra work when replacing the wattle and daub panels. The four upper gables feature quadrant bracing, quarter circles of oak making a pattern when arranged together. Both are characteristic styles of the West Midlands and are intended to demonstrate the wealth of the farmer. Blakesley Hall in Yardley shows very similar styling. Above the door is a clue to the farmhouse's owners. Carved into the moulded timber, along with the date, is a triangle of initials 'ABR', being Ambrose and Bridget Rotton. Their curious name (and spelling) pops up again in Rotton Park Road, Edgbaston. Note, too, the lead 'fire mark' (a fire insurance company emblem) on the smaller gable.

When active, the farm would have had an impressive view of the distant industrial forges of Digbeth. Over the centuries, the city has encroached on and stranded the building, variously making it a shed in a railway yard, a storage space, and in later years, offices for a techno label and a swingers' club – an occupancy that ended with a mysterious fire. However, the timbers survived the blaze and the house continues to act as a distinctive landmark for bus drivers and motorists as they turn on to the Middle Ring Road.

Address Stratford Place, Highgate, Birmingham B12 0HT | Getting there Bus 50 to Stratford Place | Tip Further echoes of 17th-century architecture can be seen in Lench's Trust Almshouses on Conybere Street. The design is by Victorian architect Julius Alfred Chatwin, the great-grandfather of writer and explorer Bruce Chatwin, also born in Birmingham.

102 Strathallan Hotel

Motel shows Birmingham's enduring passion for cars

There was a time in the 1970s when Birmingham was best known nationally for its ring roads, the newly-built Spaghetti Junction, striking British Leyland workers, and the popular-but-dull soap opera *Crossroads*, set in a motel in the fictional Kings Oak. All of these claims to fame relate to cars, roads and a lifestyle based around motoring convenience. This squat rotunda on Hagley Road, in Birmingham's hotel district, isn't unique to Birmingham, but exemplifies the city's enduring fascination with automotive culture.

The hotel was developed by Dekotel Ltd, and shaped like a defensive Martello tower. A ramp takes you up to a spiral car park, which winds around a central core for the first two storeys, and light is admitted via a wall of concrete hexagon modules: key period details.

The upper floors are the guests' bedrooms. Dekotel had the outlook that the car is as much a guest at the hotel as the driver. In more recent years, drivers seem content to park outside and walk the remaining distance to their accommodation, but in 1971 this would have represented the hotel of the future, shaped around the modern businessman's needs: once inside he did not need to leave to visit the city. This insular approach to a city's individual culture and identity was then a modern new direction. Dekotels had their own restaurant, a selection of themed bars and a communal TV lounge (TVs in rooms came later). While this approach was clearly influenced by the drive-ins and drive-thrus of US culture, the architectural form owes something to Birmingham's influential Rotunda office block of 1965.

On closer inspection, the round form is actually an 18-sided polygon: cheaper to build, and a clue to the economical nature of the hotel. Arrive at dusk, and you may witness the flickering dance of light as a car spirals round the lower floors, headlamp beams escaping through the honeycomb.

Address 225 Hagley Road, Birmingham B16 9RY | **Getting there** By car, take the A456; bus 9 or 126 to Portland Road | **Tip** In a quiet Edgbaston suburb, the Church of St Augustine of Hippo occupies its own island along Lyttelton Road and is a fine example of the Gothic architecture of J A Chatwin. It also has Birmingham's tallest spire.

103 Sutton Coldfield Odeon
Art Deco popcorn palace

Of the hundreds of cinemas that once occupied city centre and suburban locations throughout the 20th century, barely a handful still survive as working cinemas. The distinctive aquiline profiles of the former picture houses can still be spotted in the urban fabric, now occupied by bingo halls, banqueting suites and carpet remnant shops. One intact survivor from the heyday of Art Deco cinema design is Sutton Coldfield's Empire, still operating as a cinema, and an Odeon until 2006.

Odeon is an important name in Birmingham's cultural history, being the nationally successful cinema chain created by Oscar Deutsche, born in Balsall Heath, who opened his first cinema in 1928. Odeon cinemas were known for using the slogan 'Oscar Deutsche Entertains Our Nation', intended as a whimsical backronym rather than providing an authentic origin of the name. In 1935, Deutsche hired Clive Clavering to design a dramatic new cinema in Kingstanding to serve the newly built housing estate. This building still stands. Clavering then designed the Sutton Coldfield cinema, before handing future cinema design work to his boss, the architect Harry Weedon. Weedon was a native of Handsworth and involved in the design of a further 250 cinemas nationally. His practice still survives as Weedon Partnerships at Harry's Yard on Newhall Street.

The unmistakeable look of Clavering and Weedon's Odeon cinemas draws from a distinct Bauhaus influence. The buildings convey a sense of an optimistic and dynamic future, with streamlined curves, bold vertical fins and tiled exteriors. They are often charmingly asymmetrical. Windows feature minimally, to maintain a dark auditorium without feeling stark. The cinema at Sutton Coldfield has an 'older sister' in Steglitz, Berlin: the Titania-Palast, itself still screening films since 1928, and bearing a distinct family resemblance.

Address Maney Corner, Birmingham Road, Sutton Coldfield B72 1QL, www.empirecinemas.co.uk | Getting there Train to Sutton Coldfield, then a 13-minute walk; bus X4 Platinum or X5 Platinum to Maney Hill | Tip Driffold Gallery at 78 Birmingham Road is a commercial gallery offering Victorian, Impressionist and contemporary paintings, housed in a 15th-century cruck framed building.

104__ Sutton Park

Urban moorland over the horizon

Birmingham's reputation for being an urban sprawl is offset by this 2,400-acre mediaeval deer park, which is just a short train ride from New Street Station. A network of trails across the park offers a wide variety of terrain, including wetlands, meadow, woodland and areas of near wilderness. Walk for just a few minutes into the park's interior, and all signs of the surrounding townscape fade away.

There's plenty of evidence of the distant past, and Sutton Park is itself a scheduled ancient monument. Its earliest purpose was as hunting ground for Anglo-Saxon royalty. Ancient Romans used the land too: a Roman road transects the west side of the park, the course of which is still visible. In the 1st century AD, this was used to take soldiers between forts in Lichfield and Metchley (see ch. 72). Charred and split pebble clusters are evidence of burnt mounds – pop-up Bronze Age saunas.

An unexpected delight is the presence of grazing wild ponies. While this may suggest ancient indigenous wildlife, the horses were actually introduced from Exmoor in the 1990s to keep the meadows cropped. During the autumn months, the park is an ideal destination for fungi foragers. There are plenty of ink caps, ceps, puffballs and other edibles, but you may need to get up earlier than the city's Polish community, who are particularly keen collectors. Obviously, make sure you know what you're collecting, for there are many colourful but poisonous Russulae, Fly Agarics and other magically inspired mushrooms. If you don't want to take any chances, there are plenty of restaurants in the vicinity, ranging from family favourites such as Toby Carvery to the more upmarket Miller and Carter steakhouse. Or, as the park contains plentiful evidence of Birmingham's earliest history, maybe The Bracebridge restaurant, in the site of Henry VIII's 15th-century lakeside hunting lodge is the place to be.

Address Park Road, Sutton Coldfield B73 6BU, www.birmingham.gov.uk/info/20089/ parks | Getting there Train to Sutton Coldfield, then a short walk | Hours Daily 9am–dusk | Tip In contrast to Birmingham city centre, many of Sutton Coldfield's early buildings are still standing, and the nearby High Street features several charming and intriguing examples from the 17th and 18th centuries.

105 Thornton Road Poltergeist

Noisy spirits in a quiet suburb

In 1981, a cluster of houses on Thornton Road, Ward End, became the sustained focus of an unknown, stone-throwing assailant. Windows and roof tiles were smashed in night attacks that lasted over three years. Police naturally suspected the culprit was a vandal with a grudge, although several neighbouring houses were involved in the attack. Residents took to caging their windows and barricading their roofs. Police hid in back gardens, were stationed on neighbours' rooftops, and set up secret cameras – but no one was ever caught.

Police observed that the potato-sized stones had been scrubbed clean and never bore any fingerprints. Ballistics experts were called in to identify the source of the missiles, and suspected a large catapult might be in play, but they were also stumped. The beleaguered householders would report that the attacks resumed as soon as the police left. Cotton discretely threaded around their garden would still be intact the next morning, despite a sustained bombardment during the night. When rumours circulated around the neighbourhood that the families were under attack from a poltergeist, TV crews reported on the case, and it even caught the attention of science fiction author Arthur C Clarke.

The events came during a period of ghostly stories in fact and fiction, taking place in ordinary domestic settings rather than crumbling gothic mansions, and felt all the more chilling for it. Many of these stories were prompted by tenants who were keen to be relocated from their humble council properties, but the residents of Thornton Road stoically weathered the attacks. Eventually the barrage subsided, and the residents finally enjoyed some peace. Short of suspecting the police themselves, the case remains a mystery. The story is still shared in the neighbourhood today. If you visit the street, please respect the privacy of the current occupants.

Address 32, 34, 36 Thornton Road, Ward End, Birmingham B8 2LG | **Getting there** Bus 95 to St Agatha's Road | **Tip** Just a stone's throw away is Glen Park Road, where in 2004, gory stories began to circulate about the 'Birmingham Vampire'; fretful residents warned of the nocturnal bitings of a man in his 20s, though neither police nor local hospitals encountered any evidence.

106__Tilt

City arcade games

Tilt begins as a café at 10am, serving up competition-grade coffee to the first arrivals of the day. Some are here for a mid-morning perk, but others visit specifically for the pinball. Some even come from other cities. This is because Tilt's fine collection of pinball machines, spread over three floors, is unmatched outside London, and its scale makes it feel like a museum as much as an active arcade. At noon, Tilt's third element begins, with the opening of a craft ale bar, featuring drafts, bottled sours and canned cocktails. The three remain active until late.

Tilt's founder, Kirk Sadler, had a simple vision: to provide Birmingham with the three things he loves most. The bold new concept intrigues those who discover it: focus on your one true passion or sample all three. Although it has never advertised, Tilt has many regulars, and being in the heart of the city means there are plenty of new customers delighted by their discovery. Birmingham now has a new breed of pinball wizards who come for the classic games, and Tilt makes a point of having the newest pinball machine on site.

The bar's look is a sunny sort of industrial, with scaffolding racks, shelves and light fixtures complementing the reclaimed wooden parquet bar front. The tables were once school desks, and are complete with the odd schoolkid scribble. A pale yellow theme and huge shop windows on two sides confound any dingy, time-free notions you might have of a pinball arcade. The beer pumps are lined up against the huge window behind the bar, proudly proclaiming what's on offer. Tilt is an arcade within an arcade, this section being the surviving part of Union and City Arcade, once a fashionable shopping spot. The green-glazed inner balconies hide sea monsters among the Celtic knots, and the pink terracotta facade features faun-like pipers, grotesques and tridents.

Address 2 City Arcade, Birmingham B2 4TX, +44 (0)121 643 1048, www.tiltbrum.com |
Getting there Train to New Street, tram to Grand Central, or various buses to the city centre,
then a five-minute walk | Hours Mon–Thu 10am–11pm, Fri & Sat 10am–midnight, Sun
10am–10pm | Tip Flight Club is the city centre's faux Victorian darts pub at 13 Temple
Street. Book your private group darts area at www.flightclubdarts.com.

107 Tony Hancock Memorial

Remembering the lugubrious legend

Bruce Williams' *Memorial to Tony Hancock* in Old Square is an imposing bronze and glass sculpture celebrating the life, work and memory
of the Birmingham-born comedian. With his series *Hancock's Half
Hour*, which was broadcast between 1954 and 1961, Hancock became
perhaps the most popular comic in the UK.

The distinctly noir image of Hancock is taken from his official
BBC portrait photograph, which captures his deadpan on- and off-
screen character, sitting unhappily with a cup of tea with shoulders
hunched and wearing a heavy, dark coat and hat. The subject is well
suited to Williams' work, which is usually 2-D. The likeness is made
up of rows of glass rods admitting light through the thickness of a
bronze silhouette, referencing the black and white television screen
upon which most people would have seen Hancock.

'What's on the other side?' was a commonly voiced phrase in the
living rooms of TV viewers of the last century. In the case of Williams' sculpture, the answer is a transposed version of the sculpture
you saw previously. When *Hancock's Half Hour* was broadcast, there
were only two channels, and perhaps the sculpture references these
limited options. Sadly, one joke is lost to the sculpture's contemporary audiences. Hancock's final TV series contained his best-known
comic skit, 'The Blood Donor', and originally Birmingham's blood
donation centre was situated just across the road, allowing viewers
to make the connection themselves.

Hancock's star fell after the last series. He split from his longstanding scriptwriters Ray Galton and Alan Simpson, and never recap-
tured his former popularity. He moved to Sydney in 1968 to work
on a new comedy show for Australian television, but in June that
year died by suicide. The sculpture was used to raise awareness for
the charity Turning Point, which tackles problems associated with
drug and alcohol misuse.

108 Viceroy Close Demons
The Temptation of St. Anthony sculptures

The theme of The Temptation of St Anthony has been tackled by many artists over the centuries: Michelangelo, Hieronymous Bosch, Max Ernst and Salvador Dali have all responded to the nightmarish angels and devils that plagued St Anthony the Abbot on his desert pilgrimage.

Residents of the handsome Art Deco mansion flats at Viceroy Close in Edgbaston have their own version, carved in stone by Oliver O'Connor Barrett in 1938. The main panel is mounted above the caretaker's lodge, where the assembled demons appear to be a more amiable crowd, listening intently to St Anthony as he kneels in the sands of the Egyptian desert. St Anthony is the patron saint of swine herders and accordingly, a pig can be seen being tempted by a demon with an unseen morsel while being petted by another. O'Connor Barrett's work has a cartoon-like quality, and the panel looks as though it has been lifted from a comic strip. His distinctive style appears a further 15 times around the estate in keystones above the doorways to each of the blocks of flats. The heads all lie somewhere on a scale from animal to human, with one bearded figure surely being a self portrait. Variously they weep, poke out their tongue, laugh, scowl or glare at residents and visitors to the flats, and collectively multiply the visions that appeared to St Anthony. There is a clear influence from the Moai statues of Easter Island in many of the keystones, and also from Pablo Picasso's African period.

Barrett was not formally trained beyond a short course at Fircroft, a college set up in 1909 by George Cadbury for Birmingham residents with few formal qualifications, and which still offers short adult college courses in Selly Oak. Shortly after his work in Viceroy Close, the artist relocated to New York, streamlined his name to Connor Barrett, and his primitive approach eventually gave way to a more naturalistic style.

Address Viceroy Close, Birmingham B5 7UU | Getting there Bus 61 or 63 to Sir Harry's Road | Tip The empty plinth to an 1855 statue of Robert Peel, Prime Minister and founder of the police force stands in Calthorpe Park, visible from Edward Road. The statue now stands outside the Tally Ho Police Training Centre on Pershore Road after being purloined by officers in 1963.

109 Webster & Horsfall Museum

Totally wired for three centuries

The site occupied by Webster & Horsfall has been continuously industrial since the river Cole powered a grist mill here in the 14th century. The firm can trace its origins back to 1708 when John Webster arrived in Digbeth to set up a metal working shop. It can be credited with what is perhaps Birmingham's most humble story: a company that can celebrate the history of its success working with wire, an everyday material that's commonplace to the point of invisibility, through three centuries of technological innovation.

The company specialised early on in pins, needles, fishhooks and piano wire. Experiments with drawing, heating and cooling wire led in 1848 to the production of the first spring, a breakthrough that gained immediate international demand. In 1866, the company made the armoured wire for the first transatlantic telegraph cable, 1,852 nautical miles in length. Sections of the thick cables are displayed with the reverence normally reserved for the finest jewels.

It is interesting to see the ubiquity of art here. The visually striking cross-sections of the lock coil rope are showcased as large Pop Art murals. And look for the beautifully illustrated scenes of the wire manufacturing process by Arthur Lockwood, an artist renowned for his urban and industrial watercolours of Birmingham and the Black Country. The specialist wire sculptor Rupert Till has created a contained spaghetti tangle representing the swan and horse head of the firm's heraldic crest.

The wider expanse of Tyseley Energy Park represents the future of industry in Birmingham, generating energy from waste and producing low and zero carbon transport fuels, including hydrogen, electric charging and Biogas through a collaboration among Birmingham's tech innovators, academics and scientists.

Address Fordrough, Yardley, Birmingham B25 8DW, www.websterandhorsfall.co.uk | Getting there Buses X1 Platinum or X2 Platinum to Kings Road | Hours Mon–Fri, 10am–4 pm; visits can only be made by advance arrangement | Tip A 30-foot portrait of King George V made up of four shades of brick overlooks the pocket park on the end terrace house of George Road.

110 Weoley Castle

Ruined remains of a mediaeval castle

Birmingham does not have a castle. Fine examples of castles stand outside the city in Tamworth, Kenilworth and Warwick. The moated manor house of the de Bermingham family, standing near the Bull-ring since medieval times, was demolished in 1816 (though the name lives on in Moat Lane). And unfortunately, Castle Street, an alley off High Street, refers to a pub once going by that name, now lost. However, the remains of fortified manor houses can still be seen, visible by their ruined walls and the impression left by moats.

South-east of the city centre lies the suburb of Weoley Castle, taking its name from the manor house that stood there in various forms from around AD 1100. The location is significant: in Anglo-Saxon the name Weoley translates to 'temple clearing', suggesting a pre-Christian temple once stood there. The earliest building was made of timber, and had a defensive ditch before being rebuilt in the 13th century as a red sandstone building with defensive wall, crenellations, six towers and a moat. Despite these fortifications, the low-lying land suggests they were built more as a show of wealth.

The castle enjoyed three centuries of activity and extension, featuring stables, a great hall, kitchens and a brew house, becoming a popular hunting estate and manorial court where local cases were heard. In later years, owners lived outside the Midlands and leased the house to locals, after which it suffered from neglect. By the 17th century it had become a ruin, and its walls were plundered for building materials. The construction of Dudley No 2 Canal passed nearby in the 1790s, and drew from the ruins for the construction of bridges, while the material removed to form the canal was dumped in the castle's moat. Today, the various rooms and functions of the castle are clearly visible in outline, and offer a glimpse of life from a lost era.

Address Alwold Road, Weoley Castle, Birmingham B29 5RJ, www.birminghammuseums.org.uk | Getting there Bus X21 Platinum to Jervoise Road or bus 23 to Wentworth Way, then an eight-minute walk | Tip Stone House Farm on Stonehouse Lane, now First Steps Nursery, was made from material purloined from Weoley Castle in the 17th century, with evidence that the oldest remaining part is the castle's original keep, transferred stone by stone.

111 Wren's Nest

Home of the Dudley Bug

Dudley is just about as far as you can get from the ocean, but there was a time when it lay underwater and had a tropical climate. Extensive coral reefs grew in the waters, which swam with bizarre sea life. 420 million years later, the evidence of this ancient sea world can still be seen in fossil form.

The quarrymen, who in the 18th century dug limestone from Wren's Nest for building materials, would not have known what they were seeing when they found the fossils. Whereas some people thought fossils were the work of the Devil, at Wren's Nest they were embraced as friends and named Dudley Bugs. Some Victorian quarrymen would supplement their income by selling their fossil finds in the town. What we would today call a trilobite made it on to the original Dudley coat of arms, along with a fiery lizard, but these prehistoric features were removed from the official crest in 1974.

A visit to Wren's Nest today reveals a scarred landscape hidden inside woodland, as steep cliffs spill the white limestone scree down to ground level. In some sections of limestone exposure, everything to hand is rich with fossils. It is permitted to take home a souvenir, but visitors should not break anything off with a hammer. You have the option of scrambling to the higher levels, or a more sedate stroll through the woods. Several sections of the fragile landscape are fenced off, but be aware that even the accessible areas are not entirely risk-free. If you do remain at ground level, a walk through the grasslands may reveal rarer flowers such as milkwort, quaking grass and three species of orchid. At dusk, you might encounter the seven species of bat that populate the area.

Why 'Wren's Nest'? The wren is sometimes called a troglodyte, or 'cave dweller', as it likes to hide in small holes as it hunts for insects, and the quarry is rich with suitable rocky fissures.

Address Wrens Hill Road, Dudley DY1 3SB, www.dudley.gov.uk/things-to-do | Getting there Tram to Bilston, then bus 83 to Hillside Road | Tip An example of the old Dudley crest carved by William Bloye, complete with trilobite and blazing dinosaur, can be seen on the corner of the Council House on Priory Road.

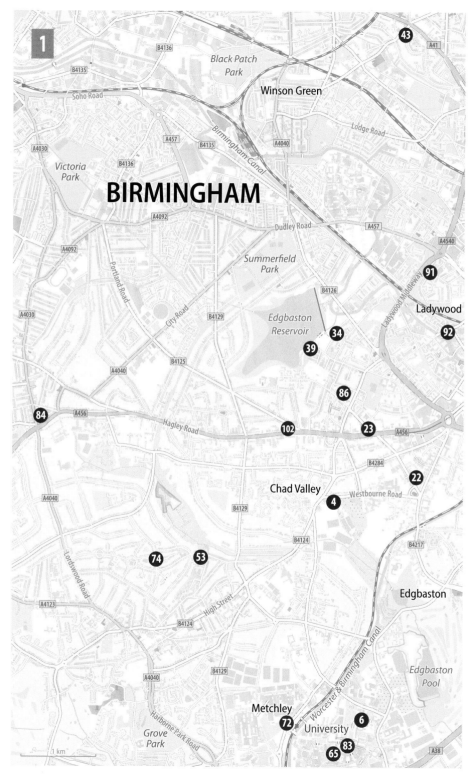

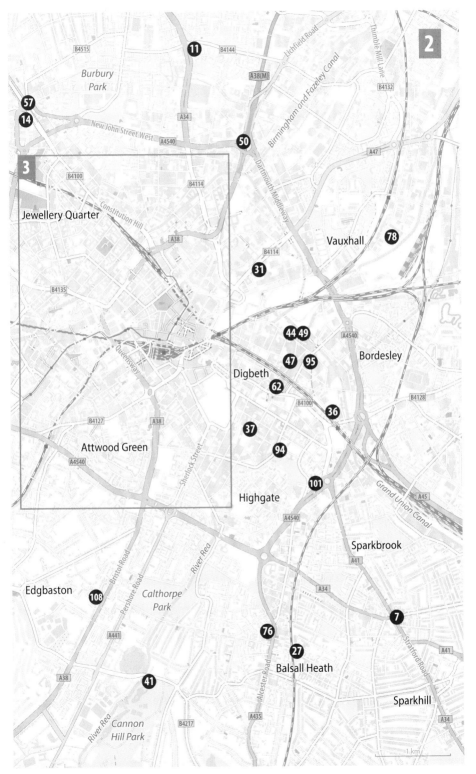

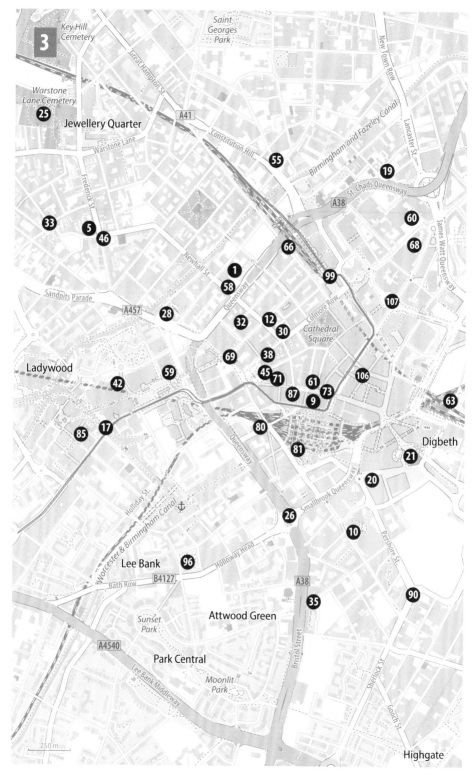

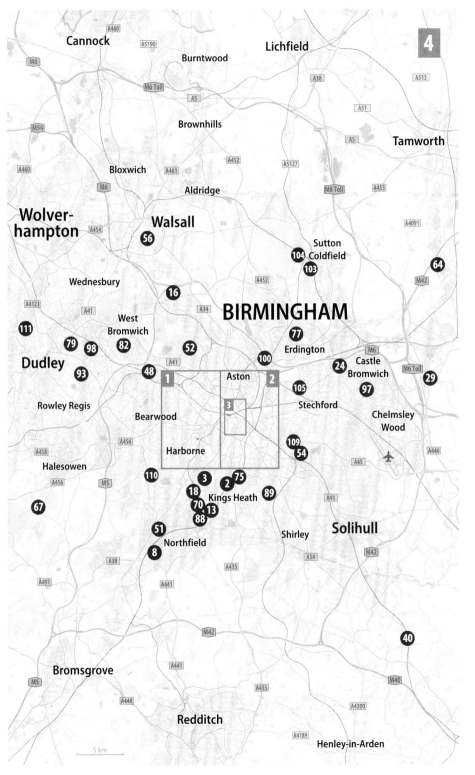

John Sykes, Birgit Weber
111 Places in London
That You Shouldn't Miss
ISBN 978-3-7408-1644-5

Ed Glinert, David Taylor
111 Places in Yorkshire
That You Shouldn't Miss
ISBN 978-3-7408-1167-9

Lindsay Sutton, David Taylor
111 Places in Lancaster
and Morecambe That
You Shouldn't Miss
ISBN 978-3-7408-1557-8

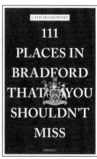

Cath Muldowney
111 Places in Bradford
That You Shouldn't Miss
ISBN 978-3-7408-1427-4

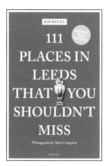

Kim Revill, Alesh Compton
111 Places in Leeds
That You Shouldn't Miss
ISBN 978-3-7408-0754-2

Michael Glover,
Richard Anderson
111 Places in Sheffield
That You Shouldn't Miss
ISBN 978-3-7408-1728-2

Julian Treuherz,
Peter de Figueiredo
111 Places in Manchester
That You Shouldn't Miss
ISBN 978-3-7408- 1862-3

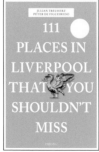

Julian Treuherz,
Peter de Figueiredo
111 Places in Liverpool
That You Shouldn't Miss
ISBN 978-3-7408-1607-0

David Taylor
111 Places in Newcastle
That You Shouldn't Miss
ISBN 978-3-7408-1043-6

Katherine Bebo, Oliver Smith
111 Places in Poole
That You Shouldn't Miss
ISBN 978-3-7408-0598-2

Katherine Bebo, Oliver Smith
111 Places in Bournemouth
That You Shouldn't Miss
ISBN 978-3-7408- 1166-2

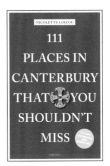

Nicolette Loizou
111 Places in Canterbury
That You Shouldn't Miss
ISBN 978-3-7408-0899-0

Rob Ganley, Ian Williams
111 Places in Coventry
That You Shouldn't Miss
ISBN 978-3-7408-1044-3

Martin Booth, Barbara Evripidou
111 Places in Bristol
That You Shouldn't Miss
ISBN 978-3-7408-1612-4

Alexandra Loske
111 Places in Brighton and
Lewes That You Shouldn't Miss
ISBN 978-3-7408-1727-5

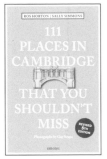

Rosalind Horton,
Sally Simmons, Guy Snape
111 Places in Cambridge
That You Shouldn't Miss
ISBN 978-3-7408-1285-0

Justin Postlethwaite
111 Places in Bath
That You Shouldn't Miss
ISBN 978-3-7408-0146-5

Gillian Tait
111 Places in Edinburgh
That You Shouldn't Miss
ISBN 978-3-7408-1476-2

Photo Credits

Argent Centre (ch. 5): photo Jonny Fuller-Rowell

Bartons Arms (ch. 11): photo Jonny Fuller-Rowell

Birmingham Opera Company (ch. 15) *Mittwoch aus Licht* photos Helen Maybanks

Bullring Meteorite (ch. 21): plaque photo Ikon Gallery

Catacombs (ch. 25): photo Jonny Fuller-Rowell

Eagle Insurance (ch. 38): photo Jonny Fuller-Rowell

Face of the Moon (ch. 43): photo Birmingham Museums Trust

Grand Union Gallery (ch. 49): photo Handover Agency

H B Sale (ch. 55): photo Jonny Fuller-Rowell

Lucifer (ch. 69): photo Birmingham Museums Trust

Museum Collection Centre (ch. 78): photo Birmingham Museums Trust

Perrott's Folly (ch. 86): photo Jonny Fuller-Rowell

Piccadilly Arcade (ch. 87): photo Jonny Fuller-Rowell

Roundhouse (ch. 92): photo National Trust Images / James Reader

Shard End Griffins (ch. 97): photo Jonny Fuller-Rowell

Weoley Castle (ch. 110): Birmingham Museums Trust

Ben Waddington portrait: Julie Oneill

Janet Hart portrait: Layla Richardson

Art Credits

A Meteorite lands in Birmingham's BullRing (ch.21) Cornelia Parker, courtesy of Frith Street Gallery

Garden of Eden and *Autumn Ramp* (ch. 30) Reuben Colley

Findings Trail (ch. 46) Laura Potter

Need Extra Cash? (ch. 47) Foka Wolf

Drye Eyes (ch. 49) Lauren Gault

Industry and Genius (ch. 59) David Patten

The Kennedy Memorial (ch. 62) Kenneth Budd ARCA

Lucifer (ch. 69) The estate of Sir Jacob Epstein

Outside-In (ch. 85) Oliver Beer

History of Snow Hill (ch. 99) Kenneth Budd ARCA

Tony Hancock Memorial (ch.107) Bruce Williams

Many people have my gratitude for the creation of this book. Thank you to all those who accompanied me on walks through four seasons to visit the 111 destinations and saw things that I didn't: Antonia Grousdanidou, Graham Dunning, Julie Oneill, Matthew Westbrook, Elvira Miceli, Ian Francis, Roxanna Collins, Matthew Cox, Alice Jones, Sherrinford Hope, Cristina Fernández Recasens, the Leopard, Raluca Vetor, Bill Sankey, Kate Gordon, Ken Searle, Heather Baseley and Chris Tomlinson.

Thanks are due to all those who suggested places to include, lent me their keen eyes, found the answers, listened, wrote and photographed inspiringly, thought through thoroughly or otherwise gave their support to the venture: Ikon Gallery, Glynis Powell, Gordon Wallace, Martin Parretti, Cornelia Parker, Rory Coonan, Nadine Lees, Colin Anderson, Laura Potter, Joe Holyoak, Alison Lester, Tim Hodgson, Fiona Adams, George Demidowicz, Kat Pearson, Jonathan Meades, Charlotte Swinnerton, Karsten Scholer, Jane Hanney, Robert Holland, Jill Arbuckle, Joff Illingworth, Karin Malmberg, Gregory Pearce, Paulette Burkill, Sandy Robertson, Laura Ager, Maung Maung Kyi, Cheryl Jones, Muneeb Mirza, Heidi Geppus, Andy Foster, Molly James, Dhruva Mistry, Selina Losa, Jonny Fuller-Rowell, Kate Grundy, Rob Gilbert, Adriana Minu, John Clarkson, Tricia O'Connor, Phil Smith and Jan Hart.

Thank you for reading this book and for inviting your friends to go out and explore.

Minty green teas were provided by Damascena of Moseley.

Final thanks to Laura Olk at Emons and my able and enduring editor, Martin Sketchley.

Ben Waddington is the director of Still Walking, a Birmingham-based festival with an annual programme of guided tours and walking events. His education is in Fine Art, a practice which informs his approach to curating and creating guided walks. He is also the city organiser for Birmingham's PechaKucha nights.

Janet Hart born and raised in Birmingham, Janet now resides in the Black Country. She is a commissioned and published photographer with a keen eye for documenting the historic and psychogeographic aspects of her surroundings. It is, therefore, not unusual to find her seeking out adventures, rummaging in derelict buildings, getting lost in woodland, or just simply watching sunsets with her dog and with trusted camera in hand.